AT THE HEART OF
THE WORLD

AT THE HEART OF THE WORLD

CORMAC MURPHY-O'CONNOR

DARTON · LONGMAN + TODD

First published in 2004 by
Darton, Longman and Todd Ltd
1 Spencer Court
140–142 Wandsworth High Street
London
SW18 4JJ

ISBN 0–232–52481–5

A catalogue record for this book is available from the British Library.

Phototypeset by Intype Libra Ltd
Printed and bound in Great Britain by
Page Bros, Norwich, Norfolk

CONTENTS

PREFACE

I'm told that in Ireland if you ask for the local equivalent of *mañana* you may be told that there is no word in the language that conveys quite the same sense of urgency.

I think my publisher must be echoing those sentiments. He has been urging me to complete this short book for well over a year now. It is not a weighty volume and much of it is adapted from talks that I have given on various occasions during the past few years. I have introduced into these addresses some autobiographical material. I wanted to express the 'family' nature of my Catholic faith; a faith which has always been rooted in relationships rather than in systems and structures, beginning of course with my own family and continuing in the family of the Church. At the heart of all those relationships has been a deep and abiding sense of hope and trust.

Jesus Christ promised that he would not leave us orphaned when he returned to the Father, and so he bequeathed to us his Spirit – the Holy Spirit – and his Bride, which is the Church. It is the Holy Spirit who is our comforter and our protector, and who ceaselessly assists us in the trials of this world and enables us to be disciples of the Gospel. It is the Holy Spirit who is at the heart of the Church and who is the foundation and inspiration of all Christian life.

The Church has often been in crisis, and is always in need of reformation. Through the ages the Church has lived, in a mystical sense, through a hundred deaths and a hundred resurrections. As I look at the Church in the world today, in particular in the Western world, I see the same imprint, the same pattern, of death and resurrection. In many spheres of human existence the Church seems hesitant, and poorly prepared to answer the many searching, and sometimes confused, questions asked by individuals and by society. I also see how influenced we as Christians can be by the *mores* of our times. Affluence has brought an increase in greed and in selfishness. Relativism has brought a narrowness of interest, and leads all too often to the pursuit of personal advantage over and above the common good. And I see a certain immaturity in the exercise of authority in the Church, which has yet to fully absorb and live out the lessons of the Second Vatican Council.

Notwithstanding its human failings, the Church has been the heart of my life. For me it embodies a living tradition which assures me that with the guidance of the Holy Spirit it will always remain both a hope and a light for our world. I find it hard to find adequate words to thank the Lord for the faith that I have been given.

The challenge confronting the Church today is how best to communicate the richness and newness of the Gospel message to the people of our time. There is a balance to be achieved here. Much of what we know and learn is communicated to us in our early education, through our wider reading, and, increasingly, by the media. But there is a much deeper truth which we cannot grasp by these means, the truth about God's unlimited love for us. And this we learn in our families, in our relationships, and in the communion of believing men and women which is the Church. This is why it is so important that as Christians we should be nourished by the practice and the teaching of the Church: by the liturgy, the sacraments (especially, I believe, the Eucharist), by our contemplation before God, and by our life in the Communion of Saints, both proclaimed and, as yet, unproclaimed.

The Church must learn to be more open and transparent. We know what shame attaches to her because of the sins of her members. This is why she must always be open to repentance and forgiveness, words which are becoming increasingly unfamiliar to many in our society. For my part, I believe there is nothing to fear, and that for those who believe in Christ the future is always full of hope, and open to new life.

There are a number of people who have helped in different ways with the preparation of this book. They know who they are and how grateful I am to them. I trust that you the readers will capture in it something of my mind and inspiration, and derive from it courage and renewed hope for the journey.

CORMAC MURPHY-O'CONNOR
November 2003

CHAPTER ONE

A Pilgrim's Journey

The joy and hope, the grief and anguish of the men and women of our time, especially of those who are poor or afflicted in any way, are the joy and hope, the grief and the anguish of the followers of Christ as well. Nothing that is genuinely human fails to find an echo in their hearts. For theirs is a community composed of men and women, of those who, united in Christ and guided by the Holy Spirit, press onwards towards the kingdom of the Father and are bearers of a message of salvation intended for all. That is why Christians cherish a feeling of deep solidarity with the human race and its history.

Gaudium et Spes[1]

The words above have come to mean a great deal to me, and are the reason I chose 'Joy and Hope' as my motto when I was ordained Bishop of Arundel and Brighton in 1977. I believe that our faith in Jesus Christ and our participation in the community of believers is indeed good news. But I also believe that it is our calling to share that good news with fellow Christians, people of other religious faiths and of no formal belief, and to listen as well as to give. These others have much to teach us, and we must have the humility to learn from them. The Spirit of God is alive, present and active. Learning to be open to that light from whatever source, and being prepared for surprises, is the only genuine response to the Spirit.

To be a Pilgrim

Many years ago I went on holiday to the Outer Hebrides, that beautiful group of islands off the north-west coast of Scotland. It was partly a pilgrimage, because I wanted to visit the places made famous by their association with the missionary monks who sailed across wild and windswept seas in the sixth, seventh and eighth centuries to establish centres of Christian mission as far east as St Gall in Switzerland and as far south as Bobbio in Italy. On one of the Hebridean islands I came across a stone which commemorated one of these holy men. I read the words inscribed on it: 'Pilgrim Cormac', and underneath, 'He went beyond what was deemed possible.'

It seemed too good a quotation to ignore and I mentioned it in the Cathedral at Westminster when I was installed as Archbishop in the year 2000. It touched me deeply to discover that I had a namesake who was a pilgrim and who had had the courage – or perhaps the foolhardiness – to take risks and pursue his dream. Pilgrim Cormac presumably had little idea where he was going to make landfall, and he may not have been much the wiser when he reached his rocky destination. He reminded me of the call of Abraham: when God had said to him, 'Go', he asked 'Where?' The answer was that he would know when he got there.

Our Celtic forebears were not only pitting their wits against winds and sea but also against the unbelief of men and women who had perhaps never heard of the good news of the Gospel. The islanders of the Outer Hebrides may have shown little inclination to listen to the Word of God when Pilgrim Cormac and his fellow monks attempted to preach to them. Those monks who travelled to distant lands are role models for those of us who try to preach the Word of God in season and out of season, often attempting to communicate with people who know little or nothing about the love of God. The Celtic monks remind me of the importance of trust, and of remaining in good heart when the signs of the times seem to indicate that the message of the world is the only one that matters, with its emphasis on the 'good life', here and now.

Our lives may be easier in material terms than those of the pilgrims of old but we are on a similar pilgrimage. We, too, face peril and uncertainty. The dangers are different, but we too are called to dream of going 'beyond what was deemed possible'. We know that the only security for the journey lies in the loving hands of a God to whom we entrust our lives, in the conviction that with God all things are possible. We can be hopeful because we know what God has done in Christ in the past. After all, it is his Church, not ours; he has sustained it through much harder times than those we are experiencing, and we can be absolutely sure that God will keep his word.

The Spirit of Pilgrimage

In his book *To Be a Pilgrim,* Cardinal Basil Hume writes movingly about the spirituality of the pilgrim:

> Pilgrims are on their way to some place; there is a destination. I would find it very hard to accept that after life on this earth there is no more 'me', and nothing for me; no more 'you', and nothing for you. It would not make sense of life, and make no sense of death.[2]

Cardinal Hume speaks of the importance he attaches to the words 'pilgrim' and 'seeking' and describes the inspiration he received from the single-mindedness and simplicity of the great Northern saints such as Aidan (d.651), monk of Iona and Bishop of Lindisfarne, whose spirit lives on in those islands. Aidan was both pilgrim and seeker. He made long missionary journeys and he must have found his work extremely disheartening at times.

During the early years of Christianity pilgrims travelled to the Holy Land to visit the places which had been sanctified by the presence of Jesus, and to Rome where so many Christians had suffered martyrdom. When wars or occupation made Jerusalem inaccessible to pilgrims the traditional burial place of St James the Apostle drew pilgrims to the great Spanish shrine of Santiago de Compostela. Pilgrims continue to walk, drive or cycle to Compostela, just as they continue to travel to the other great Christian centres of pilgrimage across the world: Knock, in Ireland, Lourdes and Paray-le-Monial in France, Fatima in Portugal and Czestochowa in Poland. Every twenty-five years they flock to Rome when a 'Holy Year' is declared. In the Americas, Guadaloupe in Mexico, Aparecida in Brazil and Lujan in Argentina draw huge numbers of the faithful. It can be a life-changing and transforming experience to arrive at a great centre of pilgrimage to which one has journeyed for days or weeks. The experience is not necessarily any less powerful if the journey has taken an hour in an aeroplane!

In *The Canterbury Tales* Geoffrey Chaucer presents us with a group of fourteenth-century pilgrims travelling from London to the great shrine of St Thomas à Becket at Canterbury. The journey was a lengthy one and it was anticipated that each pilgrim would tell four tales: two on the road to Canterbury and two more on the way back. Chaucer describes the thirty pilgrims in his prologue and in linking passages between the 'tales'. They are a motley crew. The poor country priest earns praise for his sincerity and his religious spirit but others are mocked for their pomposity and worldliness.

Pilgrimage has always been important for me. In Rome, where I trained for the priesthood, I did not have to go very far to visit some of the holiest places in Christendom. I had just arrived when in November 1950 Pope Pius XII defined the doctrine of the Assumption of the Blessed Virgin Mary into heaven at the end of her earthly life. This took place during a Holy Year which inspired millions of pilgrims to converge on Rome. I had come to the English College in October. As new students we went into retreat for a week, and then were more or less ignored for a while as all the other students were out showing pilgrims around. It was at about this time that people could begin to travel again after the war, and they came to Rome in droves. Eventually even the new students at the English College were needed to show pilgrims around the city. I had a busload to take care of and knew almost nothing, so while the pilgrims were getting out of the bus to look at a monument I would dart around the corner ahead of them to mug up the next bit of information from the guide book. I tried to pass it on to them with the aplomb of a seasoned Roman tour operator. It was even worse when two of us had to take a busload of pilgrims to Assisi. We were in a complete panic trying to find out everything about Assisi without ever having been there.

On the day of the definition of the doctrine of the Assumption I was in St Peter's Square as part of the biggest crowd I had ever seen in my life. It stretched from St Peter's right down to the Tiber. I was with a fellow student, Anthony Kenny, who many years later became Master of Balliol College, Oxford. Pius XII loved these huge gatherings. The Mass was going to take place in St Peter's Basilica and you had to have a ticket to get in. Seminarians didn't get tickets for these sorts of events, but fortunately for us the Swiss Guards on the doors of St Peter's didn't appear to know what the tickets were supposed to look like. We went round to the side entrance, produced some papers out of our pockets and announced that we were secretaries to Cardinals. They let us in and we attended the Mass in the basilica, as well as the proclamation outside in St Peter's

Square. The impression that remained with me from that day was of the universality of the Church. It was at once powerful and very moving.

I also have a wonderful memory of going on pilgrimage to San Giovanni Rotondo, south of Rome on the Adriatic coast. We were going to meet the saintly Capuchin, Padre Pio, who has since been canonised. I spent ages trying to prepare a general confession of my life in Italian, but the queue was so long that I never got into the confessional. I had been very careful about what I prepared because Padre Pio was supposed to be able to read hearts and would know if you were leaving things out. I probably should have told him that I had got into St Peter's Basilica under false pretences! But at least I managed to meet him and it was something I will never forget. More recently I have been on walking pilgrimages with groups of young people, and it has been a marvellous experience. It can be so much easier to talk about things that matter if you are walking along together.

To Travel Hopefully

The importance of pilgrimage does not lie in the destination alone. In the words of the Scottish novelist, Robert Louis Stevenson, 'To travel hopefully is a better thing than to arrive.' His fellow Scot, the Jesuit Gerard W. Hughes, describes the experience of walking from England to Rome in 1975 in terms of response to inner need.

> [Pilgrimage] is a symbolic gesture, a search for our real destination, a kind of sacramental journey, a sign that we are in search of an answer to our deepest longings, and the journey is undertaken in the belief that there is an answer.[3]

So many of us are in search of an answer to our deepest longings. We live in an age of unprecedented choice, and yet the exercise of choice is often restricted by a subliminal agenda to which our desires are unconsciously tailored. Every time we make a choice we can feel more hedged in than before. We are encouraged to buy, subscribe, insure, re-insure, invest, prefer. Such choices are important, but are they always real choices made in response to genuine need? Are we responding to movements that arise in our hearts and minds, suggestions that come from our true selves? Or are we merely responding to the blandishments of advertisers and our natural desire to possess and then to safeguard our possessions? Are we journeying into freedom, or are we retreating into dependence? Not the natural dependence of childhood; but the potentially darker dependency of an adult life in which we are unaware of our chains because they are invisible to us.

Pilgrimage is a response to the deepening call to freedom, and the true pilgrim embarks on the journey in a spirit of trust. We may not be quite sure how we shall get to our destination, or what we shall find on arrival. But we know that we are going to a holy place; that in a sense we are going 'home' – to a home that in some mysterious way responds to our most profound hopes and our deepest longing.

A Pilgrim Church

When I first heard the Church described as 'the pilgrim people of God' I thought the expression rather odd. It was not at all the way in which I had experienced the Church during my childhood and youth. The Church of my early life somehow gave the impression of being above the tumult of life. There was a sense of timelessness and invulnerability, almost a sense of imperviousness to whatever was going on in the world outside. I arrived in Rome in 1950 as an 18-year-old student for the priesthood; I remained there, with the exception of one visit home, until I was ordained in 1957 and returned to work as a priest in

England. In 1962 the Second Vatican Council gathered in Rome, and the Church was to be shaken to its foundations. When Pope John XXIII convened this great ecumenical gathering he attributed the idea to a sudden inspiration from the Holy Spirit. He defined the task of the Council as the renewal of the life of the Church, which should be brought up to date in its teaching, discipline and organisation. The ultimate goal was the unity of all Christians.

These were heady and exciting years. Rumour was rife. What had Bishop X said to Cardinal Y? Who was 'in' and who was 'out'? Could it possibly be true that the Mass would no longer be celebrated in Latin? For those who wanted to get an idea of what was really going on behind the scenes the distinguished American writer and journalist, Robert Blair Kaiser, provided outstanding coverage in *Time* magazine and went on to publish a book entitled *Inside the Council*.[4] Kaiser opens his book with the story of the Florentine painter who visited Pope Hadrian VI (1459–1523) to show him a masterpiece which he had entitled 'The Barque of Peter'. The picture showed Peter's boat lifted high above the waves by trumpet-blowing angels. Around and under the boat the waves were whipped into fury by storms and the water was full of drowning sinners. Hadrian sat high on the prow, wrapped in contemplation. The Pope is said to have been horrified by the picture. 'This is not my ship – put it on the seas, fill the sails, dip the rudder into the sea and let me steer the bishops and their flocks and be saved with these drowning heretics, schismatics and sinners.' Pope John XXIII was perhaps acting in the spirit of Hadrian when he expressed his longing to throw open the doors of the Church and declared, with an astounding open-mindedness for those times, that 'the whole world is my family'.[5]

Kaiser maintains that until Pope John convened the Second Vatican Council the Catholic Church had remained very much the barque depicted by the Florentine painter –

riding above the waves, safe, secure and well-organised. Pope John arrived with little more than an oar on his shoulder and a spark of intuition in his heart. He decided it was time to lower the boat back into the water and sail the high seas again. It was as if the Church suddenly seemed to become aware that she was caught up in the fast-flowing tide of history: that we were all pilgrims together on our way to the same destination in the fullness of the Kingdom of God.

The great French theologian, Yves Congar (1904–95) described the twentieth century as 'the century of the Church'.[6] And as the Second Vatican Council evolved we became increasingly aware of the truth of his words. I have always been convinced that we must trust Christ's promise to Peter that 'the gates of hell shall not prevail' (Matthew 16:18) and that his Church would survive.

When I was studying in Rome in the 1950s I still perceived the Church as somehow being above the waves and the tumult of life and even in some sense beyond and outside the ebb and flow of history. The Church, we were taught, is the partial realisation of the Kingdom of God on earth. It was the 'Church militant' now, and would become the 'Church triumphant' in heaven. The Roman Catholic Church was the Body of Christ, a visible institution, an organised society in which each person had his or her place. It was this institution alone that was the continuation of the Church founded by Christ: 'Thou art Peter, and upon this rock I will build my Church' (Matthew 16:18). We all knew where Peter was. He was twenty minutes' walk from the English College on the other side of the river Tiber.

I gradually began to discover, however, that while that image of the Church contains much truth, it is not the whole truth. We need other images or models, other approaches and insights in order to grasp something more of the mystery of God at work in his people. There is no way in which our limited perception can grasp the fullness of the truth of Christ and his Church. In the words of St Augustine, 'God is always more'. The true mystery of the Church is far beyond our comprehension.

As the pilgrim people of God the Church shares the fears and hopes of her brothers and sisters. She seeks to speak God's word of love 'at the heart of the world'. Pilgrims are also seekers. We seek to know the ultimate purpose of life. Why are we here? Where have we come from? Where are we going?

Cardinal Hume quite rightly turned the quest upside down:

> It helps if we switch from the notion of our searching for God and instead think about God coming to find us, for after all that is the way it is. It is we who are lost. It is God who is looking for us.[7]

In the words of St John, '[God] first loved us' (1 John 4:19). This is of vital importance for our understanding of the phrase, 'pilgrim people of God'. Jesus Christ is God's word of love to us, and God does not go back on his word. If we seek God as a pilgrim people it is because God is already looking for us. In a sense, we have already found God, and God's word of love has already been addressed to us, even if we are not conscious of having heard it. On his pilgrimage to Rome in 1975 Gerard Hughes discovered that the fact he was searching for God was a sign that God had already found him.

The word 'people' implies that the pilgrimage is not just a private understanding between me and God. We are made in the image and likeness of God, loved individually and personally by God to a degree that we cannot begin to imagine. But we also belong to one another as brothers and sisters called into the unity of God's family, which is our eternal destiny.

Pilgrim Popes

The pilgrim journeys of recent popes are striking examples of post-Vatican II outreach to the entire human family. In 1870 the remaining territorial possessions of the papacy were absorbed into the former kingdom of Italy. Pope Pius IX withdrew into the Vatican and he and his successors were initially regarded as 'prisoners in the Vatican'. For a long time the young Italian state prevented the popes from moving around freely. The Lateran Treaty between Pope Pius XI and Fascist Italy created the 'Vatican City' as a separate state. Even so it was not until the papacy of John XXIII that popes began to move beyond the Vatican and their summer retreat at Castel Gandolfo. Pope John began his papal travels within Rome. He visited the Santo Spirito Hospital and the prison of Regina Coeli, each of them a few minutes away from the Vatican.

He made history on 4 October 1962, becoming the first pope for hundreds of years to go on pilgrimage. He set out for Assisi to pray for the success of the Second Vatican Council at the tombs of St Francis (d.1226) and St Clare (d.1253), two of the greatest saints in the history of Christendom. As part of the same pilgrimage Pope John visited the Italian Shrine of Loreto near the Adriatic coast, a sanctuary associated with Mary, the Mother of Jesus, and visited by as many as six million people every year. The Council was due to open a week later on 11 October 1962.

A few weeks previously Pope John had learned that he was suffering from cancer of the stomach. He had confided to the Belgian Cardinal Leon-Joseph Suenens of Malines-Brussels (1904–96), 'my personal part in the preparation of the Council will be my suffering'.[8] Notwithstanding the short time he had left there is no doubt that his opening speech to the assembled Council Fathers was decisive in pointing the Council in the direction in which he wished it to proceed:

> The substance of the ancient doctrine of the deposit of faith is one thing, and the way in which it is presented is another. And it is the latter that must be taken into great consideration with patience if necessary, everything being measured in the forms and proportions of a magisterium which is predominantly pastoral in character.[9]

The Pope emphasised the ecumenical nature of the Council by declaring that

> the Catholic Church . . . considers it her duty to work actively so that there may be fulfilled the great mystery of that unity which Jesus Christ invoked with fervent prayer from his heavenly Father on the eve of his sacrifice.[10]

I can imagine that at least one paragraph of his opening address was a cause of consternation to some bishops, although it must have delighted others. Speaking in the plural first person, as was the custom of the times, he told them:

> In the daily exercise of our pastoral office, we sometimes have to listen, much to our regret, to voices of persons who, though burning with zeal, are not endowed with too much sense of discretion or measure. In these modern times they can see nothing but prevarication and ruin. They say that our era, in comparison with past eras, is getting worse, and they behave as though they had learned nothing from history, which is, none the less, the teacher of life. They behave as though at the time of former Councils everything was a full triumph for the Christian idea and life and for proper religious liberty. We feel we must disagree with those prophets of gloom, who are always forecasting disaster, as though the end of the world were at hand.[11]

The attentive and respectful way in which Pope John listened to the views of the different bishops during the Council was evidence that his view of the role of the Pope differed from that of some of his predecessors and, no doubt, from the views of some of his advisors.

On the death of Pope John in 1963 Cardinal Giovanni Battista Montini was elected as Pope Paul VI. He promised to continue the Second Vatican Council and within three weeks of his election had convened the second session.

Paul VI followed the example of Pope John in other ways. As the first pope to make extensive journeys overseas he was even more of a pilgrim pope. Christianity was no longer focused upon Europe but had become a truly global reality. The Pope attended an international Eucharistic conference in Bombay in 1964. In 1965 he addressed the General Assembly of the United Nations in New York. He visited Uganda in 1969 and the Philippines and Australia in 1970. Paul VI carried the message of the love and peace of God around the globe. In January 1964 he visited the Holy Land where Paul and the Ecumenical Patriarch of Constantinople, Athenagoras, embraced each other in Jerusalem. This extraordinary gesture of love and forgiveness between the leaders of two Christian Churches led to an even more remarkable act of reconciliation. On 7 December 1965 a joint declaration was read in which Paul VI and Patriarch Athenagoras declared their mutual regret for the events of 1054, when Cardinal Humbert of Silva Candida and Patriarch Michael Cerularius of Constantinople had excommunicated each other.

Pope Paul VI's vision of his call and his ministry showed him to be a worthy successor to his great patron, 'Paul, the Apostle of the Gentiles'. These remarkable words are in many ways typical of his approach to his mission and the spirit of pilgrimage in which he travelled the world:

Woe to me if I do not preach the gospel! I am sent by Christ himself to do this. I am an apostle, I am a witness.

The more distant the goal, the more difficult my mission, the more pressing is the love that urges me to it. I must bear witness to his name: Jesus is the Christ, the Son of the Living God. He reveals the invisible God, he is the first-born of all creation, the foundation of everything created. He is the teacher of mankind, and its redeemer. He was born, he died and he rose again for us. He is the centre of history and of the world; he is the one who knows us and who loves us; he is the companion and friend of our life. He is the man of sorrows and of hope. It is he who will come and who will one day be our judge and – we hope – the everlasting fullness of our existence, our happiness. I could never finish speaking about him: he is the light and the truth; indeed he is the way, the truth and the life. He is the bread and the spring of living water to satisfy our hunger and our thirst. He is our shepherd, our guide, our model, our comfort, our brother.[12]

Of all modern popes, Pope John Paul II is, of course, the one who has been most conscious of his responsibility to be physically present as pastor, not only to the *Urbi* (the city), but also the *Orbe* (the world). He has seen himself, not just as a pilgrim but as a *pontifex,* in the true sense of that word, a 'bridge-builder'. He has tried to build bridges between the different denominations of Christianity, between the Church and other faiths, and between the Church and our world.

In warning the East not to capitulate to the materialism of the West Pope John Paul has proved himself as outspoken a critic of Capitalism as of Communism. He has constantly called the attention of 'the north' to the poverty and needs of 'the south'. In his visits to Africa and to Latin America he has manifested an unflagging commitment to justice and human rights and has been undeviating in his condemnation of every kind of violence.

In ecumenical terms he has built on the foundations of

Paul VI. On a visit to Istanbul in 1979 Pope John Paul attended the Orthodox Liturgy, while the Ecumenical Patriarch attended Catholic Mass celebrated by the Pope. In 1986 he joined the Chief Rabbi at prayer in a Roman synagogue which, I suspect, made him the first pope since St Peter to worship in a synagogue. On 16 October 1986 in Assisi he led the representatives of twelve world religions in a day of prayer for peace. Robert Runcie (1921–2000) was present as Archbishop of Canterbury. He told me afterwards that when the Church leaders boarded a bus to go down to the Church of the Portiuncula in Assisi the Pope was one of the last aboard. There was no obvious seat for him and he had to walk up and down the aisle looking for a place. Archbishop Runcie saw this as genuine evidence of the way in which Pope John Paul saw his relationship with other Church leaders – he was one among them, not one to be regarded as in any way superior. Pope John Paul's meetings with Muslim leaders and with the Buddhist Patriarch of Thailand have been notable for their atmosphere of respect and goodwill, not least because of the Pope's respect for the contemplative tradition of the great religious faiths of the world.

John Paul II has proved himself a true pilgrim pope. I think particularly of his pilgrimage to Canterbury in the footsteps of the fourteenth-century pilgrims of Geoffrey Chaucer's *Canterbury Tales*. I am still deeply moved to think of Archbishop Robert Runcie and John Paul II kneeling together in prayer in Canterbury Cathedral, both reverencing the Sacred Scriptures, the Word of God – each one a sincere pilgrim on the road towards full Christian communion between our presently divided Churches (a subject I discuss in a later chapter). Pope John Paul II has richly deserved the title of a pilgrim pope 'who went further than was ever deemed possible'.

The Love of God

The pilgrimages of great popes may seem a long way from ordinary daily life. It is easy to feel that our own, perhaps humdrum, existence is a far cry from pilgrim popes and pilgrim people, giving heroic witness to the uttermost ends of the earth. But we too are pilgrims. We too are called by God, loved by God wherever we may find ourselves. And some of us may find ourselves in situations in which we feel that we are very far from the love of God. If this is the case then be assured that it is precisely when we feel furthest from God that God is in fact longing to call us to himself and overwhelm us with his love.

If we have never paid much attention to God, because life has been comparatively easy and we have never felt we needed him, it is easy to think that it is in some way 'too late' or 'not fair' to start turning to him now when things are going against us. The story Jesus tells of the prodigal son has much to teach us here. The son had fallen as low as it was possible to go. He was feeding the pigs. It is hard for us to understand how degrading that would have been for a Jew of the time of Christ. It was unthinkable to associate with anybody who was feeding pigswill to swine. To get some idea of the feelings of Jesus' listeners try to imagine the revulsion generated by the most serious and anti-social criminal or sexual behaviour today. That would have been the reaction of the audience when Jesus told them that the prodigal son had been taking care of the pigs. A *frisson* would have run through the crowd, and yet Jesus goes on to tell us that the father does not even rebuke his son for his misbehaviour. Instead, he throws his arms around him, calls for the best robe and arranges a huge 'welcome home' party. Jesus is telling us that this is the way that God the Father longs to welcome each one of us when we come to him miserable and downtrodden.

I imagine that there have been times when most of us have felt like the prodigal son – not quite sure what awaits us at the end of the journey. But that is where God will find us and where we shall find God. Our personal circumstances may not seem very glorious; our daily activity is not perhaps the stuff that shapes history; but we may be sure that we are surrounded always by the loving presence of our God. Pilgrim Cormac probably felt pretty miserable with the wind and the rain soaking him to the skin as the autumn gales rolled in off the Atlantic and the bitter wind chilled him to the bone. And I doubt if he had a tot of whisky to warm his heart and melt the frost!

There is a delightful story about John XXIII which always makes me think about this abiding presence of God in our lives. Angelo Roncalli was elected Pope in 1958 at the advanced age of 77. On his eightieth birthday a party was given for him in the Vatican. Among all the cardinals and bishops present in the great hall, there was a little group from Pope John's home village of Sotto Il Monte in northern Italy. He went over to them and said, 'My friends, thank you for coming to see me and wishing me a happy birthday. If things were different, I would like to take you out for a meal and we could talk about old times.' Then Pope John began to muse about his own life and how he was not always able to do what he wanted.

When I left Sotto Il Monte to go to the seminary, I found that the seminary was cold and the food was bad, and I was rather miserable. I said to myself, 'Angelo, this is no place for you.' But then I thought, 'God brought me here and I must trust him.' So I stayed and I was ordained a priest. Then I became a bishop's secretary. I carried the bishop's bags and I drove him round and I did this and I did that. And, occasionally, I would say to myself, 'Angelo, this is no place for you.' But then I thought, 'God has brought me here and I must trust him.' Then I was

17

drafted into the Vatican diplomatic service and I was sent to Bulgaria! I used to receive letters from the Secretariat of State telling me whom to see, and what to say, and where to go. And I would write back telling them who I had seen, and what I had said, and where I had gone. It was all very mundane and I used to say to myself, 'Angelo, this is no place for you.' But then I reflected that God had brought me there and I trusted him. Then I became Cardinal Patriarch of Venice and I was very happy. In 1958 Pope Pius XII died and, at the age of 77, I went to Rome for the Conclave. And I said to myself, 'Angelo, they wouldn't, would they?' But they did! So here I am, surrounded by cardinals, archbishops, bishops, and monsignori, all preventing me from doing what I would like to do, which is to go out for a meal to have a chat with my family. But God has brought me where I am and I trust him. In his providence he has brought you where you are and we must all trust him. Thank you for wishing me a happy birthday.

I tell this story because surely there is not one of us who has not said at one time or another, 'This is no place for me. If only things were different.' I am sure that Pilgrim Cormac must have said it a number of times. I say it fairly frequently. Under the providence of God, there is a sense in which we do not, perhaps, have any choice. God speaks to each of us, in our particular circumstances. He both calls us, and enables us, to be of service. We are called to proclaim his love and his presence, and we do this as much by our lives as by anything we say. There is a pleasing remark attributed to the great St Francis of Assisi. His brethren apparently asked Francis about their mission and his response was 'Preach the Gospel and sometimes use words.' We are pilgrims together and there is joy in our pilgrimage because we can hope in the risen Christ who walks with us.

CHAPTER TWO

Community and Communion

*'My people' are my community, which is both the small commu-
nity, those who live together, and the larger community which
surrounds it and for which it is there. 'My people' are those who
are written in my flesh as I am in theirs. Whether we are near
each other or far away, my brothers and sisters remain written
within me. I carry them, and they, me; we recognise each other
when we meet. To call them 'my people' doesn't mean that I feel
superior to them, or that I am their shepherd or that I look after
them. It means that they are mine as I am theirs. There is a sol
idarity between us. What touches them, touches me . . . They are
a springboard towards all humanity. I cannot be a universal
brother or sister unless I first love my people.*

Jean Vanier[1]

When I was young I used to dream about what I might do
when I grew up. I thought of being a doctor like my father,
or maybe a concert pianist. I enjoyed playing the piano and
became a good amateur pianist, although I do not think I
could have made a career of it. But it was nice to dream. One
day I was out with my father when he was on his rounds in
the car. He looked across at me and said, 'What about you?
What are you going to do when you grow up?'

I replied, 'I want to be a priest.'

It just came out quite spontaneously. I don't remember being particularly aware that I had been thinking about priesthood. I suppose it was not a strange thing in a family such as mine, which included a number of priests. I had three priest uncles and my father and mother were so deeply committed to their faith that their home in Reading became a home for anybody connected with the Church. Priests would call in. Visiting preachers would be invited along. I think the parish priest would tell them that they should go out for lunch, and they would be sent round to our house. It was a place of hospitality for priests. Monsignor Ronald Knox was among them, though I was away at school, at Prior Park College in Bath, when he visited. I was at school from 1945–50 and they were tough years. Food was pretty rotten, and I remember the bitterly cold winter of 1946–7.

Two of my four brothers were already at the English College in Rome training for the priesthood so it was a real sacrifice for my parents to let another son go, but they were a marvellous pair and they did it gladly. When the time came for me to make a formal application to the bishop I decided that I did not want to apply for Portsmouth diocese which included my home town of Reading. I told my father that I wanted to be accepted for Westminster diocese. I thought London would be exciting – the big city and the bright lights – and it wasn't too far from Reading! My father said he would have to talk to Archbishop King of Portsmouth. He did, but Archbishop King would not agree to me going to Westminster. He said he needed all three of us for Portsmouth, and he wanted me to join my brothers, Pat and Brian, at the English College. He was presuming that the Rector of the College would welcome a third Murphy-O'Connor, but he was wrong. The Rector thought that two was quite enough. My brother Pat had to work hard to persuade the Rector to accept me. Reluctantly he agreed and the three of us spent a year together in the College.

The journey to Rome was my first time out of England, apart from visits to Ireland. Five of us travelled together on the train from London. Some were smarter than others. I was pretty casual, while one of the others had come from a junior seminary and was dressed in a black suit and tie. I think we must have looked an odd lot. Off we went across Europe. We slept in bunks, and had been given tickets for meals. I had my first taste of spaghetti on the train from Paris to Rome.

For seven years I lived as a student in the English College in Rome, an institution with more than four hundred years of history. The college had been founded in the sixteenth century, and for two hundred years before that the building had served as lodging house for English pilgrims visiting Rome. The College stood on a site which had originally housed a street of Roman shops and stables. I was always intrigued by the fact that the horses in these stables were believed to have pulled the chariots used for racing in the Circus Maximus. This suggestion became even more vivid for me when the great Hollywood epic, *Ben Hur*, starring Charlton Heston, was released in 1959.

It was a great excitement to find myself living in Rome, and in one of the most beautiful parts of the city. This was the Rome of Vespas, Lambrettas and Fiat 500s – the driving was more like the unforgettable chariot race in *Ben Hur* than the stately progress of family saloons in England. It was also the Rome of pasta, pizza and pavement cafés, bicycle thieves and religious institutions packed with young and idealistic men and women. It was the Rome of hot, dusty streets and the Cold War, of Communists and Christian Democrats (epitomised by Giovanni Guareschi's fictional Don Camillo and his love/hate relationship with the Communist Mayor Peppone), of the actresses Gina Lollobrigida and Sophia Loren and of the great architect

Pierluigi Nervi. Not that any of them crossed the threshold of the English College, at least not while I was there!

I was a few yards away from some of the greatest historical monuments in the world including the medieval open market, the Campo dei Fiori. The flower sellers who had given the square its name hundreds of years previously were still displaying their wares in a riot of colour and it was filled with the cries of Roman matrons inviting passers-by to try the artichokes and cauliflowers, melons and peaches that filled their stalls to overflowing. It was chilling to think that this innocent colourful market square was once a designated location for public hangings and burnings. A statue of Giordano Bruno, burnt for heresy, reminds us of an ugly era. A first century Roman temple, the Pantheon, remains one of the structural wonders of the world with its extraordinary dome, which allows the sunlight to move around the walls. The Piazza Navona retains the shape of an ancient Roman racetrack, and there is the Trevi Fountain and the Jesuit Church of the Gesù, all within fifteen minutes' walk of the College. I will never forget my first experience of the awe-inspiring magnificence of St Peter's Basilica, and the remarkable peace of the Vatican Gardens just behind.

The regime was tough. We were up at 5.30 a.m. for meditation and Mass. For meditation we had a book in Latin to help us. I did not find it much help and learnt much more about prayer from what I would call the Prayer of the Church. By this I mean the different forms of prayer used by the Universal Church which slowly became deeply rooted in my mind and heart: in the times of quiet meditation and in the prayer of silence. I was also greatly helped by the prayer of my fellow students, and of the Sisters who looked after us and were a great inspiration through their life of work and prayer. After Mass we had a tiny breakfast – coffee and a roll – then set off for the Gregorian University which was run by Jesuits, and where the lectures were in Latin. I thought that my Latin would be good enough to cope with the lectures. I had not bargained for the idiosyncratic pronunciation of some of our professors.

There would be four lectures in the morning after which we walked back to the College for lunch. Before the meal we had prayers for the Conversion of England. They were known as 'starvation prayers' because our stomachs would be rumbling. In the afternoon we went out for a walk in what was called a *camerata* – a group of four. In the evening there was study, recreation and night prayer before we collapsed into bed.

There were seventy or eighty students at the College from different dioceses in England and Wales. They were a fascinating bunch. I learnt an enormous amount from my fellow students, from Rome and from Italy: more, probably, than I learnt from my studies at the university. At the Gregorian University there were students from various religious houses and from other national colleges, including American, French, German and Scottish colleges. I spent seven years studying at the 'Greg' – three years of philosophy and four years of theology. My years in Italy were wonderfully fruitful and by the time I left I had made good and lasting friendships with fellow seminarians of all nationalities who are now scattered across the world serving as diocesan priests, missionaries, teachers, university professors and chaplains.

Continuity and Change

As I look back on those years, I am struck by the mixture of continuity and change which is one of the abiding characteristics of Rome. As students in the English College, we were aware that we were part of an extraordinarily precious tradition. Seminarians who had studied at the English College during the sixteenth century were well aware that their destiny was likely to be as a fugitive priest in England where they would administer the sacraments to Roman

Catholics at risk of their lives. The College is proud of its many martyrs. The gallery of the College chapel is filled with frescoes depicting the suffering of the College's martyrs, most of whom were hung, drawn and quartered. It was a grim scenario. I am pleased to say that we were also aware that at the time of the Reformation every Christian denomination had its martyrs who chose to die rather than forfeit their religious beliefs.

Not long ago I paid a visit to Eton College where, together with the former Bishop of Coventry, I unveiled a plaque commemorating six martyrs – all old boys of the school – from the Reformation period; four were Protestant and two Catholic. More recently I was delighted to unveil a plaque to Saint John Fisher in the Chapel Royal at the Tower of London where he was imprisoned and executed. To unveil the plaque with the Bishop of London and the Bishop of Fisher's former diocese of Rochester was most moving, and symbolic of the spirit of unity and reconciliation which continues to nourish our ecumenical endeavours.

Rome has always been home to martyrs. We were aware of the catacombs close by where early Christians celebrated the Eucharist in secret and in doing so risked their lives. This was all part of a tradition which is not something lifeless or moribund. It is a living reality: a source of life and renewal, and a continuing challenge to a renewed understanding of ourselves, where we have come from and where we are going. Rightly viewed, tradition can help us to see with fresh eyes and to understand more deeply. It is a source of sometimes forgotten, or neglected, riches and an opening to the breath of the Spirit.

This became very clear to me during my first ten years as a priest. The continuity in the life of the Church was as apparent as the continuity in my own life. The sacraments were the heartbeat or pulse of Catholic life: beginning with the welcome of babies into the life of the Christian community at Baptism. Later, when the child was seven or eight, came the Sacrament of Reconciliation, Confession as it used to be known, followed by First Holy Communion. A little later there followed the Sacrament of Confirmation which was administered during the Bishop's regular visitation to the parish. Later on came the celebration and blessing of the loving commitment of couples to one another in the Sacrament of Marriage and, for some, the experience of priestly ordination. Finally there was the anointing of the sick, and the commendation of those departing this life into the loving goodness of God.

In addition to these key events in the life of the Catholic community there was the day-to-day role of the priest as pastoral and spiritual counsellor and friend. The ongoing celebration of the Sacrament of Penance and the celebration of the Eucharist on Sunday then, as now, was at the very centre of parish life. We were called to teach the fundamentals of the faith, and to reach out in service to the wider community. This was the rhythm of life in the parish community, just as it is today.

None of this is possible without the gift of the Holy Spirit. The Jesuit theologian Henri de Lubac (1896–1991) underlines the meaning of this indispensable gift:

> The divine inbreathing which is the very source of resurrection and of life has ever appeared as the source of unity, so much so, in fact, that the resurrection of the dead can be described by the word already used for the formation of the Church – *congregatio*, congregation.[2]

A great deal was happening in the Church during the years after my ordination. Although these great events did not alter the rhythm of sacramental life, they created enormous changes in the way in which we perceived ourselves and our Church, and in the way in which we celebrated the sacraments, beginning with the Eucharist. When I was ordained there was no suggestion that the Mass would ever be celebrated in any language other than Latin. The change to the vernacular liturgy was probably the most obvious change resulting from the Second Vatican Council, but there were a great many others.

These changes, and the resulting developments, profoundly affected the lives of priests and the lives of the Christian communities to which we ministered. They affected not only the liturgy, but the ways in which our communities were organised. They touched the way in which we reached out to the wider community and, more fundamentally, they changed the way in which we saw 'the Church', and our understanding of the relationship of the Church to the wider community.

The years of the Second Vatican Council were a time when the powerful forces of renewal which had been building up in the Church over many years seemed to burst through in an unexpected flood of energy. While they were exciting and challenging years, they were also years of pain and difficulty for many people. The changes were not always transmitted in a way that was nourishing and helpful. Many people were deeply hurt, not least the priests who were 'told' that they would be celebrating Mass facing the people and celebrating the liturgy in the vernacular. I was enormously impressed at the way in which many priests who were much older than me did their best to accept the changes and implement them as constructively as possible. But having said that, there was great gain as well as loss. As far as I was concerned the years of the Second Vatican Council filled my heart with joy and with hope. The joy and the hope that the Council engendered, under the guidance of God, has encouraged and sustained me through forty years of pastoral service in the Christian community; this pilgrim community at the heart of the world.

There are many images or models which can help us to acquire a fuller understanding of God's gift to us through his Church. We need to acknowledge the debt that we owe to great theologians of differing traditions, many of whom had been concerned for many years before the Council that the modern world seemed to be bypassing the Christian Churches. Karl Barth (1886–1968) and Rudolf Bultmann (1884–1976) both laid emphasis on the Church as herald, announcing definitively the Word of God for our time in the person of Christ. Other theologians reminded us that the Church was the servant of the world, a model which was dramatically developed in the Second Vatican Council document *Gaudium et Spes*, the Pastoral Constitution on the Church in the Modern World (1965). The French theologian and scientist, Pierre Teilhard de Chardin (1881–1955), and Dietrich Bonhoeffer (1906–45) pointed out that Christ was also the Lord of those who did not profess any form of religious belief. For Teilhard, Christ was the omega point and the spearhead of the evolutionary process; for Bonhoeffer he was the 'Beyond in our Midst'. The Church therefore had also to be seen as the servant of all humanity. These various ways of looking at the Church can help us to appreciate the fact that no single image or model can fully express its mystery. Each viewpoint helps us to face the key challenges that confront the Church with fresh insight and understanding as she assumes her place at the heart of the world two thousand years after the birth of Christ.

The Church as Sacrament

There is one way of talking about the Church to which the Second Vatican Council gave particular attention. This is the concept of the Church itself as sacrament, in the sense of a sacred sign. In the words of that most central of the documents of the Second Vatican Council, *Lumen Gentium*, The Dogmatic Constitution on the Church (1964): 'The Church is in the nature of a sacrament – a sign and instrument, that is, of communion with God and of unity among all men'.[3] The Church, therefore, understands

27

herself to be the place where the presence of God in Jesus Christ can be discerned and experienced, as 'an outward sign of inward grace' – to quote the Catechism definition of a sacrament.

I find this insight enormously enriching. I am deeply aware of the 'sacramental' quality of what I see and hear when I go into parishes and meet priests, teachers, religious, parish workers and volunteers doing magnificent work in the fields of liturgy and other forms of worship, in teaching and in caring for elderly and sick members of the parish and reaching out to many people in need. This is concrete evidence of the presence and action of the Spirit of the Risen Christ. God's liberating grace is at work in our midst and it is the people of God who are agents of that sacramental sign. This is truly a marvellous witness to the love of God in our world.

In speaking of itself as 'sacrament' the Church is drawing attention not to herself but to Christ. The opening words of *Lumen Gentium* do not refer directly to the Church. In the Latin the sentence reads in full, 'Christ is the Light of the Nations'. Thus the Church reflects and witnesses to the light of Christ, that light which the Church signifies and proclaims. With the focus on Christ, the Church is described as 'the universal sacrament of salvation'.[4]

In 1985 Pope John Paul II called a special meeting of bishops to celebrate the twentieth anniversary of the conclusion of the Council and to reflect upon its significance. In the summary of the meeting we were reminded:

> The Church makes itself more credible when it speaks less of itself and preaches Christ crucified and witnesses with its own life . . . The entire importance of the Church derives from its connection with Christ.[5]

The focus on Christ rather than on the Church as the source of light and salvation is even more evident in chapter 7 of *Lumen Gentium* which speaks of 'the eschatological nature of the pilgrim Church and its union with the Church in heaven'. Dictionaries define the word 'eschatology' as 'the area of theology concerned with death and the future and final destiny of human beings and the whole world'. It is not a term that we hear very frequently in supermarkets or football stadiums, but it is useful shorthand for expressing the destiny towards which we are all travelling.

Lumen Gentium also reminds us that when we reach our final home in heaven

> the universe itself, which is intimately related to men and women and attains its end through them, will be perfectly established in Christ (see Ephesians 1:10; Colossians 1:20; 2 Peter 3:10–13).[6]

The emphasis on the mystery of the Church as sign or sacrament helps us look on the Church as the sacrament of Christ and not only as an institution. It opens up new vistas for the Church's understanding of herself and her role and focuses our attention on the person of Jesus Christ. In a document welcoming the third millennium Pope John Paul II uses strong words to remind us that Jesus must be our focus:

> Unless we follow this spiritual path, external structures of communion will serve very little purpose. They would become mechanisms without a soul, 'masks' of communion rather than its means of expression and growth.[7]

In the face of the great challenges of our time, I do not believe that we shall be saved by a 'formula' but by a person. When Malcolm Muggeridge, in a famous television interview with Mother Teresa in 1968, asked her the reason for all her work in Calcutta, she answered, 'I am not doing it for a reason, I am doing it for a person.'[8]

As previous paragraphs indicate, there are two inter-related aspects of Christian life and Christian faith – not merely inter-related, but inseparable. The encounter with

Jesus Christ is personal, but it is an encounter which is at the same time communal. If I am united personally to Jesus Christ I must also be in communion with my brothers and sisters who are personally united to Jesus in the same way. I am uniquely loved by God in a way that I cannot begin to imagine and which I can experience in its fullness only in eternity. But I am, at the same time, loved as a member of the communion or community that is the Church. And the Church in its turn is a sign and instrument of intimate union with God, and of the unity of the human race: 'God so loved the world, that he gave his only begotten Son, that whosoever believeth in him should not perish but have everlasting life' (John 3:16).

Forms of Continuity

As I look back on my life I see with increasing clarity that 'community' has been a constant and a central theme, and that it is a reality which sustains me. There are many forms of community but I wish to concentrate on the small community, and the Eucharistic community.

In Westminster diocese we launched a renewal process in 2003 which will affect every parish. The focus of the process is on the formation of small groups with a special liturgical emphasis on the seasons of Lent and Advent. In some parishes there are several hundred people meeting in small groups once a week to look at the Word of God in Scripture. How does the Word of God affect my life? What does the Lord want me to do? It is both a communal and a personal journey.

When I was Bishop of Arundel and Brighton diocese we had a similar programme. Many people told me that it had changed their lives. By sharing Scripture in a small group or community we realised more deeply how the Word of God relates to ordinary everyday life. It is not a matter of 'I have to do X or Y because I am a Catholic.' It is much more a question of responding very personally to an invitation from the Lord. In a small group there are other people to help us on our journey, and we know that 'where two or three are gathered together in my name, there am I in the midst of them' (Matthew 18:20). All renewal in the Church down the ages has happened when people have gathered together. In the twelfth century St Francis of Assisi gathered a few of his friends, as did St Clare. This was the way in which many of the great religious orders were formed. It is the same in a lively parish: there will always be a small group of people getting things going with the priest: and from there things start to happen.

As my own experience of the Church as a community has deepened both as a priest and a bishop, I have tried to foster that same sense of community in others. As Rector of the English College in Rome during the 1970s I wanted to foster a sense of community among students and staff. Today I seek to encourage and promote a sense of community in Westminster diocese. This sense of community as a sustaining reality has grown and deepened within me over the years. We are pilgrims, always searching for the way forward, sometimes able to see only a few steps ahead – but our perception tends to broaden and deepen as we journey together towards our true home and ultimate destination.

Rites of Christian Initiation

The Church's understanding of the sacraments mirrors this experience. In the Sacrament of Baptism we experience Church as community as well as Church as sacrament. When I was first ordained it was frequently the case that Baptism was a 'private' ceremony which involved only the child or adult, and their immediate family and friends. Since the Council the ceremony of Baptism and the welcome of the child or adult into the community of believers has become an increasingly communal celebration which involves a group of adults, and/or children, and the entire parish. With the advent of the Rite of Christian Initiation for Adults (RCIA), the ceremony usually takes place during the Easter Vigil, and includes reception of the Eucharist and Confirmation.

Though the Rite of Baptism for children differs in some particulars from the Rite for adults, in both forms we experience person and community indissolubly linked. In the Rite of Baptism for children, the celebrant first addresses those about to be baptised: 'My dear children, the Christian community welcomes you with great joy'. He then addresses the parents and godparents in order to affirm the reason for their presence: 'You have come here to present these children for baptism. By water and the Holy Spirit they are to receive the gift of new life from God, who is love.'

Clearly it is the role of the parents and godparents to take seriously their responsibility for the nurture in faith of the baby or child for whom they are spiritually responsible. In the case of the reception of adults into the community of believers the support and help of friends and community is very much needed, but the onus of responsibility is primarily upon the adult concerned to make the decision to join the community of believers. The RCIA is an excellent example of the reality of our communion with one another. The Rite involves an experience of preparation which takes place within a small group, led by the parish priest but also involving other committed members of the parish community. It is much more than a matter of 'passing on information', vital though this is to a realistic understanding of the fundamental beliefs of the Church community. It is also much more than just 'preparing for Baptism'. Emphasis is placed on the ongoing *formation* or growth of the individual as a member of a believing community. Specific stages in the process are marked, for example, by the presentation of the Book of the Gospels, or instruction in the Our Father. So meetings of the group are more than just occasions for learning about Catholic beliefs. They are moments during which we pray together, read Scripture, talk and share together. In this way we begin to establish sustaining relationships and grow together in the faith we are all in the process of discovering. It is a time for becoming Catholic together.

I have talked with many people and priests who accompany those preparing for full reception into the Church and I appreciate the extent to which those involved in the experience of preparation find their own faith and commitment deepened and renewed. This continual process of initiation therefore becomes an ongoing source of renewal and new life for the whole parish community.

Small Communities

This introduction into the community of adult believers is in one sense the end of a journey, but in a deeper sense it is the beginning of a whole new existence in which we will come to rely profoundly on the support of fellow believers. To some extent the way in which we live our new faith will depend upon the support we receive from those around us in our small community.

What do I mean by a 'small community'? It could be the community of our own family. It could be a particular parish or diocesan organisation, or small communities that form when people gather together to reflect on their lives, read Scripture and pray together, such as the Christian Life Communities. Whatever sort of small community we belong to, I am convinced that such groups are the promise of the future. They will be a source of new inspiration, new hope and new evangelisation for the Church. We need to experience community as a place of healing where we can rediscover our faith in the humanising experience of a group of people who share the same beliefs.

In stressing the importance of small communities I do not want to downplay the importance of the parish. But in my experience the large parish community needs the energy and vitality that comes from a variety of smaller communities, both within the parish and crossing parish boundaries. This may be particularly true in large urban parishes where it is very likely that small communities will draw their members from across the city. Parish boundaries are an important logistical consideration but we need increasingly to accept that they are not the be-all and end-all for a small community. Rural parishes can also experience a need for small communities. The risk of isolation may be considerable if an area is sparsely populated. If members of the parish only meet at Sunday Mass it can be difficult to establish a real sense of parish community.

Both parishes and small faith-based communities have to cope with the reality of the growing instability of modern life, and the increasing amount of movement between parishes and dioceses. For people moving to a new area it may be particularly important to maintain an ongoing association with a small community. This is particularly true for young people who may be obliged to move comparatively frequently, because they are studying or in search of work.

Small communities can, and should, be a source of inspiration and hope, especially in times of uncertainty and instability. With the best will in the world it is comparatively easy to 'drop out' of parish life if you are in the habit of attending Sunday Mass with several hundred others and do not know anybody particularly well. Regular membership of a small community should help ensure that this does not happen.

I am very moved by so many of these small groups. Some of them are in vows and live together permanently, such as the Little Sisters of Charles de Foucauld, who live in poor locations and do very simple ordinary jobs, just being a presence of Jesus in the factory and on the housing estate. There are also the Brothers of Charles de Foucauld, and small lay communities meeting in the spirit of that extraordinary Frenchman who became one of the principal spiritual influences of the twentieth century. Then there is l'Arche, founded by Jean Vanier, where people with special needs and their assistants live together in small houses, and the many new movements such as Youth 2000. These new movements sometimes have the springtime enthusiasm of the early Church. The whole Church is called to be a new community. As it follows this calling more consciously these smaller communities will increasing find their proper place. They will not be seen as a 'church within a church' but rather as a stimulus to the whole body.

There is the risk that in becoming very involved in a new community one might become slightly divorced from the wider church, the diocesan church, and tensions can arise. But these tensions are not new and should not frighten us. All the major religious orders experienced tensions in their relationship with the wider Church. The Franciscans did, as did the Dominicans, and the Jesuits were actually suppressed by Pope Clement XIV in the second half of the eighteenth century. But all these orders, and the Church, have survived and prospered.

The Spirit of Communion

The experience of living in community and praying and worshipping as a community is an important step towards an ever deeper experience of the mystery of our humanity, the dawning realisation that we are in some mysterious way in communion as brothers and sisters. Deep within ourselves we yearn to experience this communion more completely. This yearning will begin to draw us more deeply both into the mystery of the Trinity – the community of persons which is God – and the mystery of the Church.

We have all experienced the pain of separation, the pain of tension and conflict and the yearning to rediscover lost harmony. Parents and children long for peace in the home and we all need to feel loved and taken into account. We suffer deeply when we feel ourselves distanced, segregated or excluded. Jesus knew what it was to long for community when he prayed, 'May they all be one, Father, just as you are in me and I am in you, so that they also may be in us, so that the world may believe it was you who sent me' (John 17:21).

A culture of communion means that who we *are* prevails over what we *possess*. It enables us to experience and accept in others the similarities and the differences, the positive and the negative. Other people undoubtedly experience the negative in us, and we need to discover and to understand the light and the dark in ourselves, as well as in others. Equally we must learn to appreciate the gifts of our brothers and sisters not just as gifts in which they can rejoice, but also as gifts for us, in which we can rejoice. In the words of St Paul, 'In Christ, we who are many form one body, and each member belongs to all the others. We have different gifts according to the grace given us' (Romans 12:5–6).

Every single person has something to teach me – every single person knows something that I do not know. We need to 'make room' for our brothers and sisters, bearing one another's burdens (cf Galatians 6:2) and resisting the temptations to competition, careerism, envy, jealousy and distrust which constantly beset us.

The spirit of communion is nowhere expressed more clearly than in the Sacrament of the Eucharist: the sacrament which expresses and continually renews the communion of faith, life and witness that is the mission of the

Church. One of the major achievements of the Council, building on the liturgical and ecclesiological renewal associated with it, was the renewed affirmation of the indissoluble bond between Church and Eucharist: each a sign of our communion in the Body of Christ.

Sacrosanctum Concilium, the Constitution on the Sacred Liturgy (1963) tells us,

> Christ is always present in his Church, especially in her liturgical celebrations. He is present in the sacrifice of the Mass, both in the person of his minister, 'the same now offering, through the ministry of priests, who formerly offered himself on the Cross', and most of all in the Eucharistic species.[9]

When we receive the body and blood of Christ in the Eucharist we are building up the body of Christ that is the Church. 'The liturgy is the summit towards which the activity of the Church is directed; at the same time it is the font from which all her power flows'.[10] An intimate and organic bond exists between the renewal of the liturgy and the renewal of the entire life of the Church. As Pope John Paul II writes in his 1980 letter to the bishops of the Church, *Dominicae Cenae*, 'The Church not only acts but also expresses herself in the liturgy and draws from the liturgy the strength for her life'.[11]

This theme is further developed by John Paul II in the 2003 encyclical letter *Ecclesia de Eucharistia* (On the Eucharist and the Church), which opens with the words: 'The Church draws her life from the Eucharist. This truth does not simply express a daily experience of faith, but recapitulates the heart of the mystery of the Church.' John Paul goes on to say, 'The Church was born of the Paschal mystery. For this reason the Eucharist, which is in an outstanding way the sacrament of the Paschal mystery, stands at the centre of the Church's life.'[12]

Communion in Christ

During the past century the Church has been increasingly spoken of as the sacrament of communion in Christ. The theme of communion is a *leitmotiv* in all major dialogues through which we seek to advance on the journey towards organic unity among the Christian Churches. The dialogue between the Roman Catholic Church and the Anglican Communion, and also the dialogue between the Roman Catholic Church and the Orthodox Churches, bear ample witness to this. The Church understands herself in terms of relationship, the foundational relationship with Jesus Christ. The triune God established the Church through the mission of Jesus Christ and the Holy Spirit. Through the relationship with Jesus we are in communion with the Trinity. It is through the Son and in the Spirit that we move forward in our lifelong pilgrimage towards the ecstatic communion which will be in the everlasting vision of our eternal God.

So God's love is not something that is merely a part of his nature. God *is* love – the unbreakable and living communion between Father, Son, and Holy Spirit. And this living, loving communion which is God is most powerfully manifested in the Eucharist. We experience this through the words of consecration: 'This is my body which is given up *for* you' and 'This is the cup of my blood, the blood of the new and everlasting covenant, shed *for* you and for all.' When we, the Church, celebrate the Eucharist we are united with the Risen Lord. We are asking through the power of the Spirit to be made one with Christ in his love *for* the Father and *for* one another.

I remember years ago talking with a good friend of mine, the Scottish Franciscan priest, Agnellus Andrew, who was one of the great pioneers of an explicit Christian presence on radio and television. He worked for many years at the

BBC in London before becoming a bishop in Rome. Agnellus described Jesus Christ as the 'perfect communicator'. I thought at first that he was talking about the parables of Jesus – the prodigal son, the good shepherd, the labourers in the vineyard, and so on. Agnellus agreed that the parables were remarkable models of effective communication. But in describing Jesus as 'the perfect communicator' he was referring to the fact that we find in Jesus 'an absolute communication or giving of self in love'. He described the self-giving of Jesus as communication in the deepest sense.

In reflecting on these words I began to see what he meant. In the original Latin, the word 'comm-uni-cation' signifies the act of sharing in common and thus enjoying union with. It follows, therefore, that total communication, the perfect giving of self in love, is in fact a full communion of the persons concerned. And that brings us back to the Trinitarian presence: the love of God which is in fact the existence of God in three persons through whom the inner life of God is revealed to us.

God's love for us is uniquely revealed in the Eucharistic sacrifice which promises the complete enjoyment of God for eternity, and orients us towards the union among the divine persons, and the union among the sons and daughters of God. This is underlined in *Gaudium et Spes* in the chapter 'The Community of Humankind':

> The Lord Jesus, when he prayed to the Father, 'that all may be one . . . as we are one' (John 17:21–22) opened up vistas closed to human reason, for he implied a certain likeness between the union of the divine persons, and the unity of God's sons and daughters in truth and charity. This likeness reveals that human persons, who are the only creatures on earth which God willed for themselves, cannot find themselves fully except through the sincere gift of themselves (cf. Luke 17:33).[13]

If all human persons are made in the image and likeness

of God our relation to 'the other' is not something 'added on'. It is integral to our being. The implication of the words quoted above is that we are fully and completely ourselves only when our lives are fully 'in communion' with one another in truth and love and thus with the Trinitarian God.

I had an uncle who was a priest. At family gatherings he would enjoin us to 'remember the rock from which you are hewn'. That 'rock' is, ultimately, the unbreakable dynamic and living communion of persons that is God. Some of the Greek Fathers of the Church loved to describe the triune God as 'persons in communion'. My destiny and yours is to 'discover ourselves through the gift of ourselves' and thereby to share together a life of communion with God. We may feel ourselves to be weak and wretched failures, but we are weak and wretched failures who need to help one another along the road to that fullness of communion.

At the Last Supper Jesus gave to his friends the bread and wine which had been changed into his body and blood. He called upon them to 'Do this in memory of me'. When the community of his disciples celebrate the Eucharist 'in memory of Jesus', we not only remember, but we enter ever more deeply into his dying and his rising. The brothers and sisters for whom Jesus gave his life are our brothers and sisters. When we share in his death and resurrection we share in the gift of sacred communion together with our brothers and sisters in Christ. In trying to live our lives more completely with Christ we must pray for the gift of his Spirit that our lives may be a continuous expression of the words of the Third Eucharistic Prayer: 'May (we) be filled with his Holy Spirit and become one body, one spirit in Christ.'

CHAPTER THREE

Being Faithful

Jesus calls his followers to love one another as he loves them; not just to love others as one loves oneself. He proposes something new; to love others with the very love of God; to see them with the eyes of the Lord. And we can only see and love them like that if we have experienced Jesus loving us with a liberating love. It is only then that we can open ourselves and become vulnerable and grow into greater openness to others.

Jean Vanier[1]

When I returned to England from Rome in 1957 as a newly ordained priest I was appointed to a poor parish at the north end of Portsmouth, and my eyes were opened. In seven years in Italy I had only one holiday back in England. Rome had taught me a great deal, but it had not done much to prepare me for working in Portsmouth. I was not the only student to experience culture shock on returning to England from Rome. The same is sometimes true in reverse for students arriving to study in Rome. When I returned to Rome again in 1971 as Rector of the English College we had a student from Lancashire who had a great love for his home town of Burnley. After he had been at the College for a few weeks I invited him to come and have a talk about

how things were going. 'How are you settling down, John?'
I enquired. 'How are you finding life here?' 'Well', he replied
disarmingly, 'Rome isn't a bit like Burnley.'

Rome wasn't a bit like Portsmouth either. As a newly
ordained priest I discovered that it was all very well feeling
confident about the mission to England when you were
relaxing at the English College summer villa in the verdant
hills south of Rome. It was quite a different matter when
faced with poor people struggling to raise families with very
little in the way of income or material possessions. At that
time the north end of Portsmouth was home to workers
from the naval dockyard and to the families of men serving
in the Royal Navy. Although the area was spared the scourge
of large-scale unemployment, both the dockyard and the
Navy were very gradually being run down. There was a pal-
pable feeling of hardship about the parish. Raising a family
on six pounds a week was a constant struggle. Parents lived
in real fear that the onset of long-term illness would leave
the family to survive on inadequate sickness benefit. This
constant feeling of insecurity left its mark on people.

Despite this, in general people were uncomplaining about
their hardships and there were strong networks of mutual
support within the parish. The sense always seemed to be
glass-half-full rather than glass-half-empty. Jumble sales
seemed to typify this spirit and were a highlight of parish
life. Usually there would be a queue stretching two hundred
yards outside the door of the parish hall. When the doors
opened, parishioners (and non-parishioners) would rush in
to get whatever was going at the lowest possible price – and
on occasions without paying at all!

During these years I developed a much keener awareness
and understanding of the importance of the Church's social
teaching, and the need for real involvement in the nitty-
gritty of people's daily lives. An important aspect of the
gospel of Jesus, his 'hands-on' connection with the lives of
ordinary people, came alive to me. Something which came

to be described as Christ's own preferential option for the poor.

Living Community

In 1962 I moved from north Portsmouth to Fareham, a huge parish which included five or six villages and occupied most of the area between Portsmouth and Southampton. It was here that I became aware, and then convinced, that as Christians we need to meet outside the context of the Sunday Eucharist in order to pray together, to listen to the Gospel, and to discover more deeply how the Gospel relates to our ordinary daily lives. My belief in the renewing and regenerating power of small communities, and groups meeting around the Word, began among the people of Fareham over forty years ago, at a time when the Church was embarking on the most decisive renewal in four hundred years, spearheaded by the Second Vatican Council.

I remember very well the experience of enthusiasm and then disappointment as I prepared with my fellow curate for what Fareham's parish priest had billed as a parish 'renewal'. I had been very fired up by an influential and rather controversial book by the theologian Yves Congar on the importance of lay people and their role in the Church. I was hopeful that the parish 'renewal' would be a real opportunity for the people of the parish to renew their faith, their sense of community and commitment to each other. My fellow curate and I were dreaming of a 'living parish'. Sadly it transpired that the parish priest had a rather more limited objective in mind, which was to increase the size of the Sunday collection.

Nevertheless it was clear that many people in the parish yearned for deeper spiritual nourishment. We decided that the key was to find a way for people to meet together to share their faith more deeply. We began ten sharing groups in the parish, each of which brought together between ten and sixteen people out of a congregation of a thousand people. Before long we had more than two hundred men and women meeting regularly – it had become a living parish! I attended five of the groups and my fellow curate attended the other five. These meetings had a profound effect on me. I experienced at first hand people bonding together as friendships deepened and trust grew. The groups began to revitalise the whole parish. A powerful sense of community was created. Together we began to understand the meaning of the Gospel message in a more real and living way and to experience the ways in which God was speaking to us in our daily lives.

Some of the meetings brought together young married couples and the experience of spending time with them did a lot to open my eyes to the realities of marriage and of family life. It was a source of immense encouragement for couples who were struggling to live with the stresses and challenges of married life to meet with other couples in similar situations. As I listened to married couples talking about their lives I began to discover a new dimension to my own vocation as a priest. I realised that the witness of these (sometimes struggling) married couples was sustaining me in the purpose and meaning of my priestly vocation. Likewise the presence of a priest alongside them in their sharing, and the fact that I could speak about faith and the truth and inspiration of the Gospel message from a different perspective, seemed to be a real encouragement to them on their journey.

I shall never forget the joys, the sorrows and, indeed, the tragedies in their lives. On one occasion a young couple returned home at the end of one of our meetings. The husband was on the night shift and having dropped off his wife he immediately set out again for work. On the way to work he was involved in a serious car accident and was rushed to hospital. An urgent message was brought to me at the parish house and I spent the night at the hospital with his wife waiting for news. In the morning the doctor came to tell us that her young husband had died and she was left with the agony of her bereavement and the prospect of bringing up her young family without their father. It was a terrible sadness, but also a profound privilege to be asked to share in the desolation of the family and particularly of the wife who had been left alone, suddenly and tragically, with the responsibility of bringing up and providing for three small children.

I am a passionate believer in the institution – the Sacrament – of marriage. For me it has been a great privilege to have witnessed, and to have played a small part in, so many marriages both in good times and in bad. It is important not to be too judgemental about marriage – it is something that is lived through day by day, year by year. You cannot capture the essence of a marriage with one snapshot in time. It involves a lifelong commitment and a lifetime of change and renewal. Some marriages seem destined to be easier than others: if thirty-five per cent are made in heaven, another thirty-five per cent are a real struggle. And, sadly, another thirty per cent may break up for one reason or another. I encountered all of that in Fareham and I found it both humbling and formative. I miss the ongoing contact now, most especially with young married couples.

The lifelong commitment of a man and a woman to each other in love is vital not only for themselves but for all of us. Their love is a privileged reflection of the love of God for everyone. There is a sense in which we are all in this together. We are co-responsible (a word that expresses the way in which we can live the life and the charism of the Church) as the People of God. We all need each other – married, single and celibate – and we are the poorer without one another.

It seems to me therefore that much greater effort should be given over to the building up and sustaining of married life. We all have a responsibility for this – as Church leaders, trained counsellors, work colleagues, family and friends. Marriage is not just the story of two people. The very fabric of our society is at stake, and too often we seem to be more concerned with facilitating the supposedly 'cost-free' termination of marriage than supporting and assisting couples who are experiencing difficulties in their relationship.

As for our children, there is plenty of research to support the belief not only that marriage provides the greatest possibility of stability for children, but that the love and commitment of a happy marriage is itself the best foundation upon which the children can build stable relationships in their own lives as they mature. It is a model that we reject, trivialise or disparage at our peril.

Forgiveness and Affirmation

At the heart of every marriage there needs, of course, to be constant forgiveness and affirmation. This is true of every relationship of love. In the unfolding of a marriage there is the need for continual movement away from resentment and towards a deeper unity. It has to be 'give and give' rather than 'give and take'. The lifelong relationship of married love presents a tremendous challenge to each person who is prepared to enter into this incredible experience of a total giving of self. I believe the same to be true of religious vocation. The many hours I have spent listening to married people have taught me a great deal not only about the reality of marriage but also about the reality of my own vocation.

All of us know what it means to fail to be faithful and true to the promises we make before God, whether in marriage, in the ceremony of priestly ordination or in the solemn profession of religious vows. The only honest response we can make, and that can make some amend, is to say a heartfelt,

'I'm sorry, please forgive me'. If we do not already know it, we shall soon discover that that 'sorry' will need to be said not seven times or seventy times, but seventy times seven (and that may only see us through the first few months!).

I sometimes wonder if the reason that so many have turned away from marriage and, indeed, from religious vows, is the fear of letting go and trusting in unconditional love. Is it possible that part of the reason for the failure of so many marriages is the fact that we have lost our sense of forgiveness, lost the sense that it is possible to be truly and unconditionally forgiven when we have done something that we know to be wrong?

At the heart of God's love for us, God's delight in us, there lies an inexhaustible well of mercy, compassion and forgiveness. These three qualities are inseparable and they are integral to the nature of God. Love, compassion and forgiveness are integral also to the Christian calling, and most especially to the vocation of marriage. Marriage is a call to open our hearts to the re-creative power of the inexhaustible love of God. It is a call to allow our relationships to be transformed by the redemptive mercy and healing of God. All this is lived out amid the difficulties and ordinariness of daily life.

The decision to marry is a solemn one and represents the first step on a voyage which is to be the journey of a lifetime. It is not a question of the church 'telling' people what to do, or how to live their lives. But there is no doubt that the Church and society bear a responsibility to assist and support marriages, a responsibility which we neglect at our collective cost.

If we truly value marriage we have to do much more to provide support for married people. Good preparation is crucial and the Christian churches are becoming increasingly aware of their responsibility in this area. It is sad that the same cannot always be said of the secular sphere. But preparation is only a beginning. Every marriage experiences times of strain and, I suspect, at least one period of very considerable stress, which may be sustained over a long period. The causes can be varied: financial problems, illness, bereavement, the challenges of good parenting, or conflicting expectations of emotional, spiritual and personal fulfilment.

Increased mobility means that many of us live at great distances from our immediate family. This does not help. The support of grandparents and the extended family is often not available or forthcoming to couples with young families in the way that it once was. Employers make increasing demands on their workforce and this can cause particular difficulties for people with children. They might pay lip service to the management mantra, 'Our most precious resource is our human resource', but they do not always recognise that their 'human resources' have families at home who are equally precious. 'Quality time' has to be spent with the family if healthy relationships are to be created and then sustained. It sometimes seems that the only thing that really matters at work is achieving targets and earning bonuses. You cannot build relationships of love on the basis of prolonged absence from home or on the purchasing power of big bonuses.

I do not want to suggest that marriages are breaking down simply because of increased economic or social pressures. It is my profound hope that we can find new and realistic ways in which people may be enabled to fulfil their work commitments in a way that is both personally rewarding and 'family friendly'. Employers need to pay more regard to the essential balance needed for healthy living and working.

We all need to take responsibility for our own life choices, and make sure that our decisions are made with our own health and personal development at heart, as well as the interests of our employer. As a society we need to find and hold that balance which will enable married couples and their dependent children to grow and develop in ways that are truly fulfilling. Our society needs to rediscover the joy of marriage and family life.

The Future

As I travel around the country I meet many people who talk with deep concern about the future of society in Britain and the health of our nation. They sometimes find it difficult to articulate this anxiety but it is hard to escape the impression that, one way or another, these anxieties touch us all. I have mentioned my own concern about the growing instability in family life, and the increasing breakdown of family relationships, and of marriage. One does not have to belong to a faith community to be deeply concerned about this. Aside from the terrible personal suffering involved, research suggests that family breakdown contributes to increased child poverty, diminished educational achievement and a greater likelihood of dysfunctional behaviour. But there are many other areas of anxiety in our society, among them an increased feeling of insecurity, the growing accumulation of personal debt, and a distrust of institutions and their spokespersons and of authority in general.

It is tempting to find someone to blame for the ills of society – the government, the media, big business, the church. In reality we must all take some responsibility for addressing our concerns and building greater trust in society: parents, teachers and young people as well as politicians, religious leaders and corporate enterprises, even if some among us carry very particular responsibility.

Throughout our lives we are constantly faced with the need to make moral or ethical choices and value judgements. Today, alongside a disillusionment with much traditional moral teaching, a new relativism and subjectivism have gained ground which are increasingly influential in individual and collective moral decisions. We seem to oscillate between a hedonistic view of what is best for society, based on doing whatever is best for me, and a deterministic view which maintains that all choice is illusory because everything is determined by heredity and social conditioning.

Faced with all this we may simply decide to abdicate our personal responsibility, like the scientist working in the field of human cloning who when asked about the morality of the procedure he was carrying out in his laboratory replied, 'I am a scientist, not a moral philosopher.' He was content, he said, to get on with his work and leave moral judgements to others. He might describe this as delegation. It sounds to me more like abdication. It is like choosing to walk into a vast moral maze having deliberately left your traveller's guide and (moral) compass behind. It is simply not good enough just to 'hope for the best' when one is making decisions on behalf of the rest of humankind.

In his book *The File* the distinguished academic and journalist Timothy Garton Ash describes his return to post-Cold War Berlin to examine the file which the East German Security Police, the Stasi, had kept on him. Ash made a point of talking to some of the people who had informed on him, decent people caught up in a closed system which they had come to regard as inevitable and inescapable. In that system it was taken for granted that because the survival of the State was a kind of absolute, deceit and betrayal of others were inevitable features of daily life.

Ash rejects this supposed absolute as a perversion. At the end of the book he reflects upon the moral choices which may face his own children in the fight for what he believes is 'the relativity of our own ways and beliefs'. He suggests that an awareness of this relativity makes for tolerance, and agrees with the philosopher Isaiah Berlin that 'to realise the relative value of one's own convictions and yet stand for them unflinchingly is what distinguishes a civilised man from a barbarian'. But Ash goes on to probe this presumption more deeply, tackling what he calls the underlying challenge posed by this acceptance of the relativity of values and beliefs:

> From what source can we derive those standards of right and wrong strong enough to challenge, if need be, the very system we have been brought up to accept as right and to counter the deep normative power of the given? Where to find the courage to defend these values 'unflinchingly', even to death, if we know all along that they are only relative?[2]

In the telling words of Pope John Paul II, 'You can't live provisionally, you can't die provisionally and you can't love provisionally.'[3]

The traditional Judaeo-Christian response to Ash's question is to point to the existence of an objective moral code implanted in our human nature: the so-called Natural Law. Isaiah Berlin's description of Einstein's thoughts on the issue puts it rather well:

> Moral and aesthetic values, rules, principles, cannot be derived from the sciences, which deal with what is, not with what should be; but neither are they . . . generated by differences of class, culture or race. No less than the laws of nature from which they cannot be derived, they are universal, true for men at all times, discovered by moral or aesthetic insight common to all men, and embodied in the basic principles [not the mythology] of the great world religions.[4]

Gaudium et Spes puts it another way:

> In the depth of their consciences men and women discover a law which they have not laid upon themselves and which they must obey, a law which always calls them to do good and shun evil and which when necessary speaks clearly to their hearts and says: do this; shun that.

The fact is that men and women have within their hearts a law written by God; their dignity lies in obedience to it and they will be judged accordingly. Conscience is the most secret core and sanctuary of human beings where they find themselves alone with God, whose voice can be heard in their inmost being.[5]

The Law Within the Heart

Such apparently uncompromising language of rules and principles, law and judgement can mislead us into thinking of objective morality as a set of prohibitions arbitrarily imposed by God or by an authoritarian Church with the apparent object of curtailing human enjoyment. As Christians we can sometimes encourage this misunderstanding by the moral attitudes we strike and by the language we use. The reality is quite the reverse.

The starting point for an understanding of the Christian concept of the 'law within the heart written by God' is a consideration of human happiness. What is most likely to lead to human happiness and fulfilment? In addressing this question the Christian believer is, of course, proceeding from a conviction that human life, the universe and all it contains are gifts from the hands of a Creator who brought them into being and sustains them. The Christian also believes that the correct analogy for the relationship between this Creator and his creation is that of a loving Father with his children, and that the journey upon which these children are embarked is intended to lead them ultimately to a fuller life in God. To enable them to reach that goal God has given them, not a set of prohibitions but a map; and with that map the compass which we call 'conscience'.

The cornerstones upon which the Christian moral tradition is based follow from this understanding of the nature of the created universe and the place of humanity within it. It is assumed that we are all caught up in the mystery of God who is our end and our beginning; that each human life has an inalienable dignity derived from God in whose image and likeness we are made; that we should strive to behave towards one another as we believe God behaves towards us, with justice, gentleness and generosity; and that we are the stewards of what God has created, not its owners, and are answerable to him for our stewardship.

It is easy to see the source of the Christian requirement to practice social justice; the requirement to husband rather than to squander or destroy the resources of our planet; the requirement to remain faithful within marriage and to respect the absolute value of every human life. Far from being arbitrary or irrational constraints, such precepts are profoundly positive.

Christian morality is therefore rooted in the words of Jesus (drawing on Deuteronomy 6:5 and Leviticus 19:18), 'You shall love the Lord your God with all your heart, with all your soul and with all your mind. This is the greatest and first commandment. The second is like it: You shall love your neighbour as yourself' (Matthew 22:37–9). It is a distortion of the truth to perceive Christian morality as obsessed with laws, duties and the fulfilment of obligations arbitrarily imposed by a God who is primarily concerned with law-enforcement and meting out punishment to those who offend. We see this very clearly in the parable of the prodigal son. Where the son feared judgement, he found only tears of joy and thanksgiving.

Happiness and Fulfilment

The great thirteenth-century Dominican theologian, Saint Thomas Aquinas, tells us:

[Morality] is not about what is my duty or about my obligations, but in what does happiness consist for human beings, built as we are with minds that seek to understand, hearts that long to love and be loved, and bodies that express this outwardly.

According to Aquinas everything goes back to the desire for happiness and fulfilment. We all want to be happy. The question is, what is really fulfilling, what promotes our best interests, our true good? How do we make the decisions that promote true well-being for ourselves, for our society and for our world?

Of all the questions put to Jesus during his life on earth, the most poignant and personal is perhaps that posed by the wealthy young man: 'What must I do to inherit eternal life?' (Mark 10:17; see also Matthew 19:16). What choices must I make to secure my personal destiny as a human being, in order to be truly and freely myself? Jesus answered, 'You know the commandments: you must not kill, you must not commit adultery, you must not steal' (Mark 10:19), a teaching summed up in, 'You must love God with all your heart and your neighbour as yourself' (see Matthew 22:37–9). In the Old Testament the good life, in every sense of the word, meant that one was rich and possessed land where one could live in freedom and righteousness. With Jesus, the good life means something different. The promise for those who keep the commandments is the Kingdom of God, and possession of the Kingdom is always beyond the horizon. Yet even here and now the reality of keeping the commandments can bring meaning and hope into life. For me the commandments should be read and lived in the light of the Beatitudes (Matthew 5:1–12). If we reflect upon what it means to be poor in spirit, pure in heart, gentle and merciful, and on what it means to work for justice and peace, then we discover the true meaning of the commandments and how they lead us to the Kingdom of Heaven.

I am constantly heartened by the strong desire among so many people to live a better life, and to help others to live fuller, richer lives. This is very far indeed from being an impulse exclusive to religious believers. But for those of us who follow the teaching of Jesus we come back to the question of the rich young man: 'What must I do to inherit eternal life?' Jesus looked at him with love and said: 'Go, sell what you own, give the money to the poor and come, follow me' (Matthew 19:21). Jesus looks at each one of us with love. For most of us it is not possible to give up all our material possessions in order to follow Jesus. But in the story of the rich young man we are told that if we are to inherit the Kingdom of Heaven we cannot allow material things to come first. There is a hierarchy inherent in human values. The sincere search for truth and meaning, for peace of soul, for hope in the future, for communion with the poor and the disadvantaged and for the small joys of daily life among those who surround us, has to take precedence over our more trivial and selfish desires. It may sound idealistic, but here on earth we are called to create a garden of Eden where justice and peace will reign, and in which the poor and the marginalised are recognised as somehow at the heart of our world.

The challenge for each of us is the same whatever our station or circumstances in life. Jean Vanier puts it well:

Jesus calls his followers to love one another as he loves them; not just to love others as one loves oneself. He proposes something new; to love others with the very love of God; to see them with the eyes of the Lord. And we can only see and love them like that if we have experienced Jesus loving us with a liberating love. It is only then that we can open ourselves and become vulnerable and grow into greater openness to others.[6]

To begin to live with this openness of heart, in the spirit of the beatitudes, is the call of every Christian. I also believe that this moral map is available to all people of good will, whatever their religious beliefs or lack of them, should they choose to use it. By listening to the deepest promptings of our heart, we are all able to hear the voice of conscience, and begin to find the path to happiness and fulfilment.

CHAPTER FOUR

Openness of Heart

Here is my secret. I tell it to you with an openness of heart that I doubt I shall ever achieve again. I pray that you are in a quiet room as you hear these words. My secret is that I need God – that I am sick and can no longer make it alone. I need God to help me give, because I no longer seem to be capable of giving; to help me to be kind, as I no longer seem capable of kindness, to help me love, as I seem beyond being able to love.

Douglas Coupland[1]

As a young priest I spent a lot of my time working with young people. I was not particularly good at it but I very much enjoyed the experience. In Fareham we had a youth club with a membership of between 30 and 50 which met in the school hall, and invariably got me into a lot of trouble with the school head and with the caretaker. One evening I invited a youth club from Winchester to visit us. It was not a great success. The two groups failed to jell. The Fareham young people decided that the Winchester lot were snooty, and things rather went on from there. In the end I had to break up a fight between two of the lads with the one from Fareham protesting, 'But Father, he's trying to pinch my girl!' I can't remember the reply from Winchester. I like to think that I have learned a thing or two since then.

It was the age of the Beatles – 'Twist and Shout', 'Yeah, Yeah, Yeah!' The youth club went mad over them for the first couple of years. I must say I was pretty keen on them too. When Sue Lawley invited me onto Desert Island Discs I chose the Beatles' 'Yesterday' as one of the eight records I would take to my desert island; not that my troubles have ever seemed 'so far away'.

Two of the youngsters in the youth club played the guitar. I could also play and there were two sisters in the club who sang really well. There was a competition for Christian youth clubs in Hampshire to see which one could compose and sing the best Gospel song. I wrote a song called, 'Come Ye Blessed of My Father'. It wasn't particularly good but we sang it rather well and managed to get through the preliminary rounds of the competition. Later we were invited to join eleven other groups at Beaulieu Abbey near Southampton for the finals. The winning group was to be decided partly by the judges and partly by the applause, rather like *Pop Idol*. I don't know whether it was by design or by accident but our group brought along much the largest crowd of supporters. So when we sang the applause was deafening and we came first.

Listening to Young People

I have always found it tremendously encouraging to be with young people. There can be no Church without the young: they are an integral and vital part of our Christian community. In speaking to parents I often mention that it is not just parents who love their children – God loves them and the family of the Church loves them and cherishes them. I would not say that young people are always the easiest of interlocutors. But they are sharp and they do not miss too many tricks. I believe that they have much to say to the Church, and much that bishops need to hear, and want to hear. We should listen more to St Benedict, who told us in the sixth century that 'God often reveals what is better to the younger'.[2]

The popular caricature of the teenager and the young adult as great talkers but not very good listeners is unfair. The truth is that they just manage to look as though they aren't listening. They are saturated with input from a variety of sources so it sometimes takes time to download and process the different messages. In my experience young people are, in fact, very attentive listeners. I often wonder how good we are at listening to them. One way in which we can help them is by just allowing them to talk – to think aloud – without saying too much ourselves; without feeling that we have to rush in every time they come up with some remark or observation with which we disagree. We also need to be able to meet them where they are, rather than where we think they ought to be.

During my first term as an 18-year-old student at the English College in Rome I remember returning from the Gregorian University to the College one morning with three other students. We decided to break the rules and go into a bar. We ordered cups of coffee and cream cakes and sat down in a corner. A smart-looking priest walked into the bar. He was wearing a short cape – a *ferraiolo* – so we realised he must be a bigwig. He drank a cup of black coffee and then, spotting three students, came across to us. We felt a bit sheepish because everybody knew that students weren't supposed to go to bars. He did not rebuke us but just shook our hands, welcomed us in very poor English and said that he hoped we would have a very happy time in Rome. As he was leaving he added, 'My name is Monsignor Montini.' That was my first meeting with the future Pope Paul VI. He could have said: 'I ought to tell you that you shouldn't be in a bar', but his first word was a welcome greeting. That was very typical of Paul VI. It is so important when dealing with the young to be able to welcome them – to meet and to see the person rather than the potential problem or the misdemeanour.

Later when I was Rector of the College I used to take bishops to visit Paul VI. They always came out of his study completely transformed. 'Abbot Basil' came to stay with us at the English College in 1976 as Archbishop-designate of Westminster. It would be putting it mildly to say that he was in a bit of a state. He didn't know if he had done the right thing in accepting the job, wasn't sure if he was the right person for it, and in all was very apprehensive. I took him to meet Pope Paul and left them together. When Basil Hume came out of the Pope's study he was a different person. Pope Paul had welcomed and affirmed him. The role of Peter is to confirm and strengthen his brethren (Luke 22:32) and Pope Paul was able to do this. It is not just bishops who need strengthening and confirming – we have to keep this constantly in mind in our dealings with the young.

I suppose it goes without saying that young people are more in touch with the changing tempo of the times than the middle-aged and the elderly. This does not mean they have a monopoly on common sense or wisdom (far from it); but it does mean that they have a crucial role to play in the serious dialogue which must take place between the Church and the modern world. They are sensible enough to know that they cannot do everything on their own, and for many young people today the authority of the peer group is perceived as very much stronger and more significant than authority exercised from 'on high'. This can be good, but there is also a need for the wisdom of experience. It is imperative to listen, and I think we are learning to do this. Many more bishops would now feel open to dialogue with young people than was the case when I was young. As far as my own contacts with them are concerned, I try to build in opportunities to meet with the young – to listen to them, learn from them and share with them. I believe it is important actively to create opportunities for young people to encounter Jesus in a personal way. If you come from a Christian home you cannot just adopt the faith of your parents: it has to be appropriated, to become your own way of seeing and living.

When it comes to matters of faith and morals young people are looking for witnesses to the truth. We have to be witnesses as well as teachers. This is a difficult challenge for the Church, but it should also be an invigorating one. If I do not live out the truth that I teach and in which I profess to believe then my witness is false. If my false witness leads someone into sin then Jesus has a stern warning: 'If anyone causes one of these little ones who believe in me to sin, it would be better for that person to have a large millstone hung around their neck and to be drowned in the depths of the sea' (Matthew 18:6).

There is a powerful moment in the ceremony of the ordination of a deacon when he is given the book of the Gospels and enjoined to 'Believe what you read, teach what you believe and practise what you teach'. This is Christ's command, a call to the deacon to bear authentic witness. The extent to which there is convergence between belief, practice and teaching is a sort of litmus test for society and for the young it is the benchmark of authenticity.

Towards the end of his life St Francis of Assisi was challenged by a peasant who was concerned about the need to practise what one preaches. Francis was travelling with his companions towards the mountain retreat of La Verna, which had been given to the friars by a rich man. It was a place of deep significance for Francis because it was here that he had received the marks of the five wounds of Christ imprinted in his hands, his feet and his side. Francis was only in his forties but he had become so weak that the brothers asked an elderly peasant if he would lend his donkey for Francis to ride. With great care the good man saddled the donkey, led it to Francis, helped him into the saddle and walked beside him. As they were going along, the peasant enquired, 'Are you Brother Francis of Assisi?' Francis replied that he was. 'Well then,' said the peasant, 'try to be as good as everyone thinks you are because many people have great faith in you. So I urge you, never let there be anything in you different from what they expect of you'.

When Francis heard these words he got off the donkey, threw himself on his knees and thanked the peasant for having admonished him so charitably. I think that St Francis is probably my favourite saint. I love that story because it shows that even the greatest saints have to remember that their gifts come from God. They too have to be humble, and subject to challenge and to correction.

Bishops and other Church leaders need to take note of this. It is a good thing that young people today regard us as people rather than hierarchs. I find it both humbling and curiously liberating to recognise that in the eyes of the young our teaching authority and our ability to evangelise derive from the authenticity of our personal witness rather than the authority of office. There are of course other aspects to the *magisterium* or teaching authority of the Church and I shall explore these towards the end of this book. It would be unrealistic and unfair to expect a young person to possess an instant appreciation of the complexities of Christ's gift of authority to his Church. If they were able to grasp it they would still expect congruity among belief, teaching and practice. In order to have any chance of reaching them, we must practise what we preach. Our approach to the young should surely be one of respecting their generosity and their intuition while expecting to be asked awkward questions that probe our integrity.

The Challenge of Postmodernism

Some time ago a group of European bishops were invited to Rome to meet with a number of youth leaders in order to explore 'the ways and means by which the Christian faith places itself within the living fabric of contemporary culture, unleashing within it the renewing energy and newness of the Gospel'.[3]

The seminar provided an opportunity to stand back and ask some important questions:

- Is the Church really in dialogue with contemporary culture and with young people?

- Are we in dialogue with them – or are we talking past them?

- Do we understand sufficiently the fabric of our contemporary culture, and particularly the culture of contemporary youth?

- Do we recognise the vital importance of engaging with that culture in order to discover new ways of bringing the Gospel to the world?

The seminar was extremely fruitful and although we did not come up with any magic solutions the experience of contact and dialogue was immensely helpful and underlined the importance of continuing to meet: the importance of acknowledging the realities of the present world with its general distrust of grand theories and ideologies.

The culture of our modern society is sometimes labelled 'postmodern'. Postmodernism is a slippery concept, its definition hard to pin down. For most people it suggests in part a rejection of traditional values, values born (in the West, at least) out of centuries of Christian culture. My worry is that by jettisoning specific values we are in danger of dehumanising the fabric of our society.

However, as well as challenging us, postmodernism may also be liberating us. Postmodernism is new and different. It requires a new sensitivity and a fresh approach. On the one hand, the world of the 'postmodern' is witnessing the serious breakdown of some of the fundamental building blocks in our society. Our social groupings are suffering a severe loss of confidence and are under threat of disintegration; in many cases the threat has become a reality. On a more positive note, the challenging of assumptions is breathing new life into some of our more moribund institutions. It is also unmasking some of the most inhuman aspects of our society, such as child abuse.

The postmodern encourages greater individualism. When this is coupled with an increasing lack of confidence in social groupings it poses a threat to social cohesion. More seriously, it poses a threat to the basic community which is one of the fundamental building blocks of any society and one of the most vital and sensitive support systems – the family.

In an earlier chapter I expressed my belief in the importance of family and also my strong conviction that in the future we shall all need some form of 'small community'. For some people community may mean 'family' in the sense of our closest relations. But for most of us community means more than our immediate family. Most of us need these small communities, which can be places of profound human growth and development.

Christian leaders from the time of St Peter have emphasised the importance of community. In the sixth century St Benedict gave us his Rule which has been one of the cornerstones of monastic community life. In modern times, Jean Vanier of l'Arche and Brother Roger Schultz of Taizé have each given powerful witness to the vital importance of community. The experience of community is both a deeply precious and a fragile reality. It is also a genuine experience of what it means to be human. Community is an answer to the deep sense of isolation which afflicts our society.

The Need for God

Douglas Coupland's novel *Life after God*, from which I quoted at the head of this chapter, seems to me to explore both the tension and the richness at the heart of postmodernism. Coupland's is a still small voice speaking out of the desolation that can be part of the experience of so many in today's society. But is not this very isolation the beginning of our reaching out to God? Is the experience of the postmodern not in fact leading young people back to God? I hope so. I believe so. God, revealed in Jesus, is for all time. He is the sign for this age as for every other. The Church recognises and acknowledges the crucial importance of evangelising young people, so it is necessary to look very carefully at their experience. The indispensable factor in evangelisation is of course the personal encounter with Jesus. How can this come about in our world?

Personal encounter cannot be taught or manufactured, but it can be shared and encouraged. In the evangelisation of a young person, one of the most profoundly formative experiences is the shared journey of faith. Young people meet Jesus in one another. We must do everything possible to encourage opportunities for shared experiences of community and communion in our parishes and in our dioceses. Pilgrimages, fellowship groups and justice and peace activities are just three of the many possibilities.

The encounter with Jesus frequently comes about in our most desolate moment, when we are at our lowest ebb. During his crucifixion, Jesus gave himself into the hands of the Father at the moment when he felt most alone: 'My God, my God, why have you forsaken me?' (Matthew 27:46). It is in our very restlessness and insecurity that we come to Christ, asking 'Who am I?', 'Why am I?' Life can be fraught with insecurity because so much of what had previously seemed secure and absolute is now under suspicion. I believe that young people want us to meet them where they are and to evangelise them by helping them to read the scripture of their lives as they are. If they are angry then we meet them in their anger. If they are confused we need to be with them in their confusion. If they are desolate then we are called to meet them in their desolation. I would be very concerned, for example, if in our rush to evangelise we fail to respect the desolate moment.

Why is a personal encounter with Jesus more important than so much of our religious catechesis, to which it is possible to give a notional rather than a real assent? I suspect it is because today many people are suspicious of 'received truth'. There is a need to answer the fundamental questions: 'Why am I here?', 'Why did God make us human?', 'How do we know what it means to be human?' We can only discover the answers slowly; and it is in our encounter with Christ that we can make the journey of discovery. Jesus is our way. It is he himself who answers our questions and reveals us to ourselves. Jesus is the revelation of what God is like, and it is Jesus who enables us to reach the Father.

God gave us his son, a human being like ourselves, so that we can understand what it is to be completely and authentically human. He gave us his son so that we can see how Jesus lived and so that we, in our turn, can learn to love and respect others as Jesus loves and respects them. It is in this way we can learn to live as beloved sons and daughters of our Father in heaven.

If it is Jesus who reveals to us our human purpose, then the Church needs to be the secure base in which we can discover most profoundly the experience of communion which lies at the heart of our common humanity. Pope John Paul II was remarkably perspicacious about this point in his first encyclical letter, *Redemptor Hominis*:

Since [Jesus] is the way for the Church, the way for her daily life and experience, for her mission and toil, the Church of today must be aware in an always new manner of the situation of human beings . . . She must be aware of the threats to humanity and of all that seems to oppose the endeavour to make human life ever more human.[4]

More recently in *Novo Millennio Ineunte* John Paul insists upon the importance of the Church seeing herself as 'the home and school of communion'. We need, he says, to promote a spirituality of communion which

implies an ability to see what is positive in others, to welcome it and prize it as a gift from God; not only as a gift for the brother or sister who has received it directly, but also as a gift for me.[5]

This is a challenge for everybody but particularly for Church leaders. The Pope speaks of the Church as a home and it is a lovely and enriching thing when people are able to feel at home in the Church, whatever their background. It is certainly not enough to rely on them getting used to things as they are. There are various ways of helping young people to feel at home in the Church. One way which I find helpful is to make a point of trying to meet with them once a month. This provides an opportunity for them to share their unique gifts and particularly those gifts of joy, of healing and of forgiveness within a community setting. Recently I have encouraged large gatherings of young people in Westminster Cathedral and it has given me an opportunity to say a few words and then to listen to the young express their own views, hopes and experiences of Christ in the Church.

It seems to me important to rediscover faith in the humanising experience of community and to respect the fact that community is a place of healing. I have witnessed and experienced something of this myself through the service of so many young people during the annual diocesan pilgrimage to Lourdes. L'Arche is another example of a place of healing in which young people can experience enormous liberation through living alongside people with special needs. They are allowed to discover and accept their own needs, and are liberated from the pressure of appearing to be without blemish or wounds. Lourdes and l'Arche are places where the Thomas in us can put our fingers into our own wounds and into the wounds of our brothers and sisters (John 20:25–28).

Community, therefore, is enormously important in our culture, suspicious as it is of institutions and 'top-down' evangelism. Experience of a small community, especially in the period after leaving school or while at university or college, is particularly helpful. In *Novo Millennio Ineunte* Pope John Paul praises the vitality of communities and movements within the Church as 'God's gift to us'.[6] He reminds us that they represent a 'true springtime of the spirit'. And he goes on to echo the warning of St Paul: 'Do not quench the Spirit, do not despise prophesying, but test everything and hold fast to what is good' (1 Thessalonians 5:19–21).

An important test of the authenticity of our communities is the extent to which they are centred on the unique gift of every human person. Our openness to one another in love is the authentic sign of our Christian witness.

CHAPTER FIVE

Living Authority

Like the women [who saw the empty tomb] we must indeed confidently proclaim our faith. But we cannot respond to the crisis of authority just by asserting our faith ever more strongly, hammering away. For many people this will confirm their fears about the nature of Church authority, that it is oppressive and destructive of their proper freedom. We show that the Word we proclaim does not just stand over and against us. It is more intimate to our being than any word we could speak; it made us and it enters the darkest places of the human heart, and offers us all a home. Then we will be able to speak of the absolute claim of Christ with authority, and show it to offer us true freedom.

Timothy Radcliffe OP[1]

There have been times when I have found authority difficult. It was difficult, for example, to leave my rural diocese in Arundel and Brighton to come and live in London. That said, there are, of course, a great many joys about being here. London is extraordinarily cosmopolitan, and so is the diocese of Westminster. I love meeting people from so many different backgrounds and cultures. I just wish that I had more time to be the sort of pastor that I would like to be. This job is not very good for the spiritual life. The cares, and some of the worries, are considerable. I am constantly trying to keep up because there is never sufficient time. You have to think on many different levels simultaneously, while always having a concern for the good of the wider Church.

There is a passage from the writings of St Gregory the Great which we read in the Prayer of the Church on his feast day, 3 September. Gregory was the Pope who sent St Augustine of Canterbury to England in 596 to re-found the Church here, so we have a particular link with him in these islands:

> I am forced to consider questions affecting churches and monasteries and often I must judge the lives and actions of individuals; at one moment I am forced to take part in certain civil affairs, next I must worry over the incursions of barbarians and fear the wolves who menace the flock entrusted to my care; now I must accept political responsibility in order to give support to those who preserve the rule of law; now I must bear patiently the villainies of brigands, and then I must confront them, yet in all charity . . . Who am I – what kind of watchman am I? I do not stand on the pinnacle of achievement, I languish rather in the depths of my weakness. And yet the creator and redeemer of humankind can give me, unworthy though I be, the grace to see life whole and power to speak effectively of it. It is for love of him that I do not spare myself in preaching him.

I do not have to worry about the incursions of barbarians in the sense that Gregory was using the term, but there is no shortage of 'wolves' to menace the flock. The Catholic community in this country is no longer on the periphery. It is at the centre, along with other Christians. This change in the public perception of the Catholic Church has come about in no small part because the Catholic community is a microcosm of our society. Catholics in England and Wales are an extraordinary mix of ethnic groups which range from the descendants of those who came over from Ireland in the nineteenth century to the Vietnamese and Coptic communities of Westminster and elsewhere.

The reforms of the Second Vatican Council have also contributed to this new sense of connectedness between the Catholic community and the nation as a whole. The Council shifted our centre of gravity, allowing Catholics to engage more intensely with their fellow Christians and to relate to the world with a greater sense of confidence and ease. The Council insisted that the Catholic Church existed not just to be a 'city on the hill' by itself. It had a mission in the world and I think that Catholic people in this country have gradually become aware of this. Cardinal Basil Hume contributed much to the increasingly central role which the Catholic community plays in our society. He became a very prominent national figure, both by nature and by grace.

The Cardinal Archbishop of Westminster has always had to be involved with the affairs of the Church at international level in Rome, but his involvement with the affairs of the nation is a more recent development. The media like to describe the Archbishop of Westminster as 'the leader of the Catholic Church in this country', giving the impression he has authority over other bishops. This is not the case. In fact, a Roman Catholic bishop, while faithful to the Holy See, is completely autonomous in his own diocese. The Cardinal Archbishop of Westminster is no exception. He exercises authority only in his own diocese, like any other bishop. The title of 'Cardinal' has relevance in Rome rather than in one's own country because it is the Cardinals who are responsible for the election of a pope. So when I speak out about matters which concern members of the Catholic community here, I am first and foremost expressing my own opinions. However, I attempt to do so in a way that also reflects the views of the wider Catholic Church, including those of my fellow bishops and the Roman Catholic community of England and Wales. I would like the Catholic Church in this country to stand alongside other Christians, and indeed members of other faiths, as an influential moral leader placing particular emphasis on truth and on the sanctity of life.

The way in which a bishop is called to fulfil his role of service in today's world differs vastly from the way in which a bishop functioned in the world of my childhood. The task is the same, but the complexity of modern life and the demands and responsibilities of the post-Vatican II Church are very different. How can we touch people's lives? How do we dialogue with them rather than impose on them? How do we listen and speak out in ways that will make people take notice? I am sometimes asked how one learns to be a bishop. The answer is that you don't! You just get plunged into it. People who are going to be bishops go on a short introductory course in Rome, but it takes a lot more than that to become a good bishop. The wisdom of the older bishops needs to be made more available to those who are newly appointed.

The Service of Authority

This brings us to the whole question of authority, an issue which touches us all in a deeply personal way. The exercise of authority, whether in the home, at work, at school, on the street, in the church, in the mosque or in the synagogue, is a fact of everyday life. But authority makes many people instinctively uncomfortable. I think this may be in part because we confuse authority with power, and power makes us nervous. In itself this is unsurprising. People are increasingly and rightly intolerant of the abuse of power or the perceived abuse of power in any context. This of course includes the abuse of power in the Church.

Reservations about the exercise of authority are therefore understandable and with regard to any abuse of authority they are certainly justified. I think those who occupy positions of authority in the Church should explain the way in which their authority is exercised. We have to give reasons for the Church's claim to speak with authority on many of the key issues affecting society today.

The source of authority in the Church is the teaching of Jesus Christ. One of the principal documents of the Second Vatican Council, *Lumen Gentium*, includes a succinct summary not only of the purpose of the Church and the meaning and context of her authority but also the reason for the claim of the Church to speak and act with authority in the world:

> [The Church] is founded by Christ as a communion of life, love and truth; by him too it is taken up as the instrument of salvation for all, as the light of the world and the salt of the earth (see Matthew 5:13–16) it is sent forth into the whole world.[2]

Authority in the Church exists to preserve and foster the communion of life, love and truth among its members in communion with Christ. This communion is a charism, or gift of the Holy Spirit, and not merely an organisational necessity. In the words of the Bishops of England and Wales,

> Authority is not a possession, but a possession between the members of the body. The source of authority is its connection with the purpose of the whole body, the mission of Christ . . . When the communion nature of the Church is uppermost, authority can be seen in more relational terms.[3]

There is then a sense in which authority in the Church is shared among the members in the form of co-responsibility. This authority of co-responsibility expresses itself in a number of ways and, contrary to popular belief, authority in the Church is neither static nor unchanging. Neither is it analogous to the exercise of authority in other Churches, some of which look to Scripture as the sole reference for their teaching authority. Roman Catholics recognise and value the authority of Scripture, but we also recognise the authority of tradition and of the *magisterium*. The word 'magisterium' comes from the Latin *magister* (teacher). It is usually used to describe the official teaching body of the Church, in particular the bishops led by the Pope, but in fact refers to the teaching authority of the whole Church, of which the bishops and the Pope are the official representatives in apostolic succession from the Apostles and Saint Peter.

In the life of the Church authority should not be understood in terms of a dry or juridical reality. It is rather a living and constantly developing relationship with God and with the members of Christ's body, for the building up of that body, for the preservation of its unity and for the deepening of its sense of mission. When the Church is merely 'an institution' then her authority is institutionalised. When the Church is 'a communion' the exercise of authority is in the context of *communio*. This is not a diminishing of authority, but a difference in focus. Rather than seeing the Church as a pyramid with the Pope at the top and the laity at the bottom, a better image is that of a concentric circle, so that we are in communion with one another in the context of an authority which is listening and consultative. The Second Vatican Council tried to move us towards this with its requirement that the bishop should have a pastoral council (including lay members) and a council of priests. This is an attempt to bring the bishop into real contact with other people instead of functioning as a lone voice. He has to be in communion with his diocese.

There is a unique aspect to the exercise of authority in the Church and it is essential to recognise it. The Church's authority is always exercised in the context of the *sensus*

Ecclesiae, which Pope Paul VI described as an a
the Church and her mystery. This awareness i
reality which has proved itself to be extraordinarily robust
in transcending the tussles and conflicts which characterise
any human community.

Love for the Church helps us to see beyond the fractures,
disappointments and dark moments in her history to the
abiding beauty within. The community of the Church cherishes in its heart the abiding reality of Jesus Christ. The
British Prime Minister Harold Macmillan was once asked
about the most difficult aspect of his job. He famously
replied, 'Events, dear boy, events': those unforeseen troubles
that seem to come out of nowhere. The Church is not
immune to unforeseen troubles that come out of nowhere.
Neither is she exempt from the vagaries of human nature,
historical accident or Hamlet's 'slings and arrows of outra-
geous fortune'.

What is the secret of her astonishing staying power? It is
in part the strength and depth of the teaching authority of
the Church which has built up over the centuries and continues to develop. It is also her constantly deepening understanding of the mandate to fulfil in truth and love the
mission of Christ to his Church.

The Church is also gifted in possessing a living tradition
at the heart of this ever deepening self-understanding. The
Church is speaking out of this living tradition when she
speaks on matters of doctrine and morals. Through the Holy
Spirit, the living tradition conveys the learning of all the
previous centuries. This is not the handing on of lifeless for-
mulas. As *Dei Verbum,* the Dogmatic Constitution on Divine
Revelation (1965), reminds us, the entire revelation of God
is summed up in Christ, yet the tradition that comes from
the apostles makes progress in the Church, with the help of
the Holy Spirit. There is growth in insight into the realities
and words that are being passed on, so that as the centuries
go by the Church advances towards the fullness of truth

'until eventually the words of God are fulfilled in her'.[4] So tradition is a living reality of extraordinary power that transcends cultural and theological considerations and constraints. One of the principal purposes of the teaching authority of the Church is a deepening of the self-understanding of the Christian community as a community of mission: a community which can give confident witness to the world.

The Word of God

Christ bestowed upon the successors of St Peter a particular role of service in the Church. It is for this reason that the bishops, in communion with the Pope as the successor of Peter, have a specific role to hold together the people of God in truth and in sacramental worship. In communion with the Pope, the bishops have a distinctive teaching function: it is their task to interpret the Word of God in a way that is authentic. In the words of *Dei Verbum*:

> The task of authentically interpreting the word of God, whether in its written form or in the form of tradition, has been entrusted only to those charged with the Church's ongoing teaching function, whose authority is exercised in the name of Jesus Christ. This teaching authority is not above the word of God but is rather its servant, teaching nothing but what is handed down. At the divine command and with the help of the Holy Spirit it listens to this devoutly, guards it reverently and expounds it faithfully.[5]

The service of authority therefore resides in a particular way with the bishops and with the Pope. But this Council document makes it clear that the purpose of authority is *service*. I mentioned earlier the importance of co-responsibility. Priests, religious and lay people are also responsible for holding in faithfulness and truth the deposit of faith which

Jesus gave us: his gift of salvation which embraces life, loving forgiveness and the hope of eternal life. In other words, there is a call for all of us to develop our faith to the best of our ability in trying to understand the scriptural inspiration of authority in the Church and the development of that authority through time as a living tradition.

It is perfectly legitimate to differ in our views about the manner in which this authority should be used. The Church must always be open to reform and development, and it is sometimes entirely right and appropriate to question the way in which authority is exercised. Pope John Paul II recognises this and, in 1995, invited other Christian leaders to dialogue with him about 'a way of exercising the primacy which is open to a new situation'.[6] He has also made formal and sincere apology for mistakes made in the past. The Church must not be afraid to acknowledge errors in its exercise of authority and to remedy these. It would be foolish to pretend that we have a record of unblemished service in this area. The experience of recent history, as well as of the distant past, requires us to look openly and honestly at the way in which authority has been used.

A More Humble Church

In recent years the question of how the Catholic Church has dealt with allegations of child abuse, both in this country and elsewhere has been one of considerable pain and concern to me. The pain that I have personally experienced in the course of some of the media coverage of this matter is nothing compared with the pain experienced by victims of child abuse and their families. One of the most vital lessons that I have learnt as a result of recent experiences has been the importance of trying to understand more deeply the trauma, anger and pain suffered by those who have been afflicted.

I am very conscious of the extent to which the Church has failed to deal adequately with the sexual abuse of children and vulnerable adults by Catholic priests in the past. There is no meaningful excuse for the failure to protect innocent and vulnerable lives. The fact that the authorities in the Church failed on many occasions to deal adequately with allegations of abuse is a cause of great shame. Without doubt, it has undermined credibility in the witness of the Catholic Church to the Gospel of Jesus Christ. This has been all the more painful because priests, religious and lay people within the Catholic Church have contributed so much over so many years to the care of children, whether in schools, orphanages, adoption agencies, and in countless other ways. It is right that we should pay tribute to the countless priests and religious who have devoted their lives to the care of children and young people, and who have been deeply shamed and their reputations damaged by the abusive actions of a few.

I have talked in an earlier chapter about death and resurrection and about the need for the Church to be constantly reformed. The establishment of guidelines for the protection of children has brought about a sea-change in the way the Catholic Church approaches the whole area of child protection. Guidelines were laid down by the Bishops' Conference in 1994 and in 2000 the Nolan Committee was established. The legacy of that committee's Report is that we now have in place in the Catholic Church clear guidelines for the protection of children and vulnerable adults drawn up by an independent group of experts and formally accepted by the Bishops of England and Wales. Each Bishop has personally committed his diocese to their implementation. It can now honestly be said that the issue and practice of child protection is being given the very highest priority. The procedures now in place in each diocese and each parish should be second to none in their thoroughness and integrity.

The Catholic Church should be completely open in its social policies, especially with regard to the protection of children. Recent experiences have been deeply painful to me and to the Catholic community as a whole. Yet I believe we will emerge from them a humbler Church, unafraid to show before society, in clear and practical form, our love and care for children. My hope is that our experience will spur us to extend greater openness and transparency in all our policies and procedures throughout the Catholic Church.

The Church founded by Jesus does not make any claim to immunity from the consequences of human failure, nor to any artificial institutional strength. In the contemplation of her own weakness the Church can only become more deeply aware of the fact that she is supported solely through the constant, abiding and faithful love of Jesus who gave his life for her, and through whom she will grow and develop in spirit and in truth. I believe in the faithfulness of Christ to his Church and to each one of us. He promised to be with us until the end of time. Christ does not abandon his Church any more than he abandons you or me.

The Authority of the Spirit

The Church's understanding of tradition includes this ongoing experience of the fact that she has not been abandoned. It is the experience of transformation from the darkness of human brokenness into the light of our life in God. In the words of the bishops meeting in Synod in Rome in 1999:

> Even in great difficulties, when hope grows dim and faith is in crisis, Jesus is present. He does not abandon his Church but walks with her as a companion along the way . . . accompanying her with a delicacy which attests to the absolutely gratuitous character of his love.[7]

During the Mass we ask God to 'look not upon our sins but on the faith of your Church'. We are asking for the courage to trust not in ourselves but in God. He is the author, the originator of our authority. He does not abandon us, and our failures can never diminish his authority. The Gospels make it very clear that the person of Christ is central to the issue of the authentic witness and exercise of authority. From the very beginning of his public ministry the questions on the tip of everyone's tongues were, 'Who are you?' and 'Where do you come from?'. This is hardly surprising. People could see what he was doing and hear what he was saying. They wanted to know the source of his power and influence: 'Who are you?' and 'Where do you come from?' quickly turned into questions about authority ('By what authority do you say and do these things?'), and this concerned the religious leaders. If the authority of Jesus was greater than their own authority they were in trouble. If, on the other hand, Jesus was exercising a lesser authority it was Jesus who was in trouble. This issue provided the pretext for putting him to death. Jesus was perceived to be challenging either the authority of the Roman occupying power or the authority of the religious establishment. One way or the other he had to go.

But the Romans and the religious establishment were both wrong. The authority of Jesus is not like any other authority. It flows from the author, the originator, of all authority: from God himself. The unique aspect of the authority of Jesus is the fact that it reveals something that can be revealed in no other way. The authority of Jesus reveals the Father: 'To have seen me is to have seen the Father' (John 14:9). The authority of Jesus makes God present and active among us and creates for us a new covenant, a new relationship with God. It is the creative authority of the Spirit which purifies, renews and generates new understanding: an authority which reveals and which saves and is distinguished by the gift of forgiveness.

The Gift of Forgiveness

Jesus' miracles of healing were greeted with joy and amazement by his contemporaries, but it was his audacity in forgiving sin that provoked scandal and the instinctive reaction, 'This is going too far!', 'Who does he think he is?', 'Surely God alone can forgive?' In the 'Our Father', the prayer that Jesus gave us, we ask God to 'Forgive us our sins as we forgive those who sin against us'. Scandalous and incredible though it may seem, Jesus actually forgives sin in the name of his Father and in this way he reveals a power and authority which puts our earthly power games into unflattering perspective. In Capernaum the paralysed man is lowered through the roof to Jesus because the crowds are too great for the man to be carried through the door. In the House of Simon the Pharisee Jesus lovingly acknowledges the woman who washes his feet when Simon the Pharisee has neglected to offer this habitual gesture of politeness. In these and so many of the events of his life Jesus reveals the astonishing simplicity and compassion of our God, who does not conceal himself from us or from our shame. Like the good shepherd or the father of the prodigal son he reaches out to meet us where we are and as we are – weak, sinful and shamed. He forgives us and he loves us back into life.

I would like to think that the desire of Jesus to forgive could have as electrifying an effect on the world of the twenty-first century as it did on his Galilean audiences. But I have the impression that we are in fact losing any real sense of the need to be forgiven, let alone the necessity to forgive anybody else. We live in a climate of blame in which a so-called 'news story' can seriously damage a person's reputation and self-respect. There is a diminishing concern for the well-being of others, which should be one of the hallmarks of a civilised society.

I sense that we are on the edge of a cultural abyss and that we need urgently to draw back from it. Whatever our religious beliefs or lack of them, we can find considerable assistance in the wisdom of the ages, and in the writings of our spiritual predecessors. In the Judaeo-Christian culture we discover that it was the prophets who first developed the theme of the forgiveness of God. And then comes Jesus, who does more than merely tell us about forgiveness. He brings us the forgiveness of God. The insight which Jesus offers into the forgiving heart of our God is central to the Church's understanding of her own authority. She has received her authority from Christ and exercises it in the name of Christ. She must therefore exercise authority with the greatest humility and cannot allow herself to act in ways that are unworthy of the mission of service to which she has been called.

The Church has nothing greater to offer than Jesus Christ and life in his Spirit. You and I have nothing more to offer than the life and love of God revealed in Jesus. But we have a duty to offer nothing less. This presents us with a tremendous challenge. How do we fulfil such an awe-inspiring responsibility? In the tradition of the Church, the *sensus Ecclesiae,* that unique awareness in the membership of the Church and in the soul of each member is the source of great strength. Whatever our collective and individual failings, the reality that we offer to our world is the reality of the living Jesus; his gift of forgiveness and his gift of love. These are transmitted by the power of the Holy Spirit through the Word of the Father, the sacraments of the Church, and the abiding presence of God. It is the privilege of each one of us to bear them into the heart of our world in fulfilment of his great command, his great assurance: 'Go therefore and teach all nations, baptising them in the name of the Father and of the Son and of the Holy Spirit, and know that I am with you always, even to the end of time.'

CHAPTER SIX

Unity in the Truth

Love grows by means of truth and the truth draws near to man by means of love. Mindful of this I lift up to the Lord this prayer:

O Christ, may all that is part of today's encounter be born of the Spirit of Truth and be made fruitful through love. Behold before us the past and the future; behold before us the desires of so many hearts. You who are the Lord of history and the Lord of human hearts, be with us. Christ Jesus, eternal son of God, be with us.

Pope John Paul II[1]

The Christian unity for which we hope and pray cannot be compared with two companies agreeing to work more closely together but with pre-established contractual limits to the extent of their merger. It is more like a road which we begin to walk down only to find that there is no turning back. We cannot say, 'I will go this far and no further.' We begin the journey because we have experienced a vision and a union with Christ, and we long to share that vision, and to enter into union with our brothers and sisters in Christ. Pope John Paul's plea at Canterbury in 1982 was deeply moving, and affirmed the total commitment of the Catholic Church to the ecumenical path.

First Steps

My mother was probably instrumental in sparking off my interest in the possibilities for Christian unity. She was a member of 'Sword of the Spirit', which had been founded in 1940 by Cardinal Hinsley and sought to unite all people of good will against the totalitarian threat to traditional Western ideals. It could be described as the first stirring in this country of Roman Catholic involvement at a grassroots level with the movement for Christian unity, although the initial ecumenical collaboration did not progress very far. My mother was a very modern woman and much more adventurous and open to developments than my father. She saw flaws in the Church which my father would be more likely to overlook. I think women are like that over all sorts of things in the Church, and I do question whether we use their gifts of wisdom and discernment enough. These gifts are generally widely appreciated and used in our parishes, but the same cannot always be said at diocesan level or at some levels in Rome.

My mother was a great influence on me. She came from Cloyne in County Cork, as did my father, and when she married at the age of 21 she had just left University College, Cork where she had read French. This had perhaps opened her eyes to European thought, and, in general terms, ecumenism was much further advanced in Europe than in Britain. From my own point of view it is probably fair to say that the most profound ecumenical experiences of my life took place in Rome, where I lived for nearly fourteen years, first as a student for the priesthood at the English College, and many years later as Rector of the College. This may sound strange, because Rome does not generally strike people as the heartland of ecumenism. But it was in Rome that I became very friendly with an eminent minister of the United Reformed Church, Dr Norman Goodall, a friendship from which I benefited immensely at a spiritual level. In the college we all gained from Norman's deep spirituality, humanity and humour, and he told us that he, too, had been much enriched by his association with us. In his book, *Second Fiddle*, he recalls his sojourn in Rome at the College:

> With my Roman Catholic friends I found that even at points where, in respect of doctrine and ecclesiology, I had to say 'I cannot accept this', I knew without a shadow of doubt that at the greatest of all spiritual depths we belonged to one another in the confidence that we were on pilgrimage with each other and with a Lord who is leading us into a fuller understanding of the term 'one holy catholic and apostolic Church' than any of us has yet perceived or experienced.[2]

I recall too the visit of the Archbishop of Canterbury, Dr Michael Ramsey, in 1966 and his meeting with Pope Paul VI. The Archbishop and Pope Paul pledged themselves and the faithful of the Anglican Communion and the Roman Catholic Church to live and work courageously in the hope of reconciliation and unity in our common Lord. Together they affirmed

> our desire that all those Christians who belong to these two communions may be animated by the sentiments of respect, esteem and fraternal love, and in order to help these develop to the full [we] intend to inaugurate between the Roman Catholic Church and the Anglican Communion a serious dialogue which, founded on the Gospels and the ancient common traditions may lead to that unity for which Christ prayed.[3]

I seem to remember that Dr Ramsey, on leaving the College, turned round and, on receiving generous applause from the seminary students, took off his hat, threw it into the air and got into his car. He never got his hat back.

I described earlier the meeting between the Pope and

Archbishop Runcie when they prayed together at the shrine of the martyrdom of St Thomas à Becket in Canterbury Cathedral and initiated a new stage in our dialogue. As I watched the ceremony in Canterbury Cathedral tears came to my eyes. I remember thinking to myself that this is how it ought to be – past animosities and misunderstandings finished and a new communion and friendship begun for the sake of the Gospel.

During his visit Pope John Paul had a conversation in the deanery at Canterbury with a group of Church leaders gathered together there by the British Council of Churches. At the end of the meeting the Pope invited 'some of you . . . to visit Rome together with some representatives of the Episcopal Conference of Great Britain in order, please God, to build further on the foundation so happily laid today.'⁴ It was a group of twelve that responded to his invitation and I was fortunate to be among them. We set out for Rome on the Feast of St Mark, 25 April 1983, and the words of the Gospel for that day were ringing in my ears.

> And so the Lord Jesus, after he had spoken to them, was taken up to heaven; there at the right hand of God he took his place, while they, going out, preached everywhere, the Lord working with them and confirming the Word by the signs that accompanied it (Mark 16:19–20).

There were signs accompanying our visit to Rome which confirmed to me that the hand of God was upon it. The first of these was the real sense of unity and understanding of fellow Christians, and a vibrant sense of the way in which mutual suspicion could be diminished by dialogue in understanding and in love. As we sat in a semicircle with the Pope in his study in the Vatican I felt that the importance of the visit lay not only in the fact that it was the first visit of this nature but also in the ease, openness and normality of our being together with him. I thought back to *Unitatis Redintegratio*, the Decree on Ecumenism of the

Second Vatican Council (1964): 'Whatever is truly Christian is never contrary to what genuinely belongs to the faith; indeed, it can always bring a more perfect realisation of the very mystery of Christ and the Church'.[5]

'I look upon the world as my parish,' said John Wesley, the founder of the Methodist movement. During that meeting in Rome it was possible to understand in a new way that care and service of local churches by the Holy See need not detract from legitimate autonomy, but could enhance the unity and diversity of a worldwide communion. There are, however, extremely complex and delicate issues to be addressed. How precisely will the Roman Catholic Church address the question of a universal primacy in terms of the dialogue with other Christians, and how is any such primacy to be exercised?

I mentioned in the previous chapter that Pope John Paul had asked Christians of differing denominations and their theologians to dialogue with him on the subject of 'a way of exercising the primacy which is open to a new situation'.[6] This leads to a further question concerning the extent to which the structures and procedures of the Roman Curia adequately respect the exercise of legitimate authority and responsibility at different levels of the Church. It could be said that the Roman Catholic Church has a responsibility to put its own ecumenical house in order, at the same time as travelling down the road towards institutional unity with differing Churches.

The Second Vatican Council reminded us that the gifts of God are present in all the people of God. We need, therefore, to discover ways of fostering the effective participation of clergy and lay people in synodical or representative bodies within the Roman Catholic Church. This is an area in which the experience of other Christians may be of assistance. A further question concerns the extent to which the collegiality or shared responsibility of bishops has been implemented in accordance with the teaching of the

Second Vatican Council. Has sufficient provision been made to ensure consultation between the Pope and local churches before important decisions are made at international or local level? These are major questions and the answers will not be found easily or overnight.

A Difficult Road

The Church is not a kind of federation of Christian denominations, nor is it merely a gathering of individuals each following Christ within a particular Christian community and devoting themselves to evangelisation and the service of others. *Lumen Gentium* deliberately uses five or six different images of the Church, suggesting that the way forward is to hold in balance these different images rather than seeking a strict definition. The Church has an existence which both precedes and goes beyond the conscious adherence of believers to Jesus Christ, and to the particular community of which we are members. It is at one and the same time the community we build up together, and the womb that carries us: the maternal community that begets us into the life of God in Jesus Christ and through the Holy Spirit. It is in this sense that Catholics pray during the Mass, 'Look not on our sins but on the faith of the Church'. Jesus has not left us orphans, and in order to be with us till the end of time he has left us his Spirit and his bride which is the Church.

Pope John XXIII made this declaration to the observers from other Christian Churches during the Second Vatican Council: 'We do not intend to conduct a trial of the past, we do not want to prove who was right and who was wrong. All we want to say is: let us come together. Let us make an end of our divisions.' It was in this spirit that we spoke to one another and to officials of the Roman Curia during our 1983 visit to Rome. The terminology of our denominations differed. Genuine dialogue called for self-critical reflection and an effort to find words and expressions that we could all truly understand. We came together not just to talk but to listen to one another in the conviction that the Holy Spirit was speaking to all our Churches. I believe that a further sign of the hand of God during our visit to Rome was our appreciation of the value of genuine dialogue, calling as it does for mutual trust and the endeavour to understand the thought patterns of others in real love.

These experiences in Rome revealed yet again the divergence between differing visions of the Church. This is in part the painful consequence of our failure to recognise the Church as a supernatural reality that transcends us and to which we are not sufficiently receptive. We are constantly called to rediscover the mystery and reality of the Church in our midst.

Ecumenism is about our faithfulness to Jesus Christ and his Church, in whatever way we regard that Church. At the heart of the ecumenical journey is the Cross, for the Cross of Christ is the foundation of every holy and good work. The Cross is present in some of the questions which the Roman Catholic Church must address in terms of the legitimate exercise of authority. These questions must be raised and dealt with. Each of us has to pay a certain price if we are to achieve the goal which is at the heart of Christ's prayer 'that they may all be one'.

Small is Beautiful

My own ecumenical vision is a fairly simple one. First, I believe that each one of us should share our faith and live that faith more deeply. Second, I believe that 'small is beautiful'.

The ecumenical movement is sometimes perceived as the overcoming of obstacles. In fact it is just as much a matter of the sharing of gifts. The Roman Catholic Church does not believe in an 'ecumenism of return' – or 'you-come-inism' as some would describe it. We are already united in a common baptism and a love of Jesus Christ, and we are spiritually nourished not by the owning of Christ's gift but by the sharing of it. We long for the realisation of this sharing. Archbishop Robert Runcie gave an example of this in his description of an occasion when he was celebrating the Eucharist in Canterbury Cathedral during a retreat led by Jean Vanier of l'Arche:

> There was a man named Robert. We shared the same name and the same birthplace in Liverpool. A casual observer might have dismissed him as awkward and inarticulate. He presented himself in a line with those coming up for communion or a blessing. Robert seemed uncertain what he was asking for. Finally he took the host, looked at it and then broke it in two and handed half of it back to me. There could have been no better expression of the truth that we are spiritually nourished not by the owning but the sharing of Christ's gift.[7]

When we turn to Jesus together his Spirit evokes a freshness of attitude and the unstinting love which is the prerequisite of any growth in communion. There is so much that we share: not only our common baptism and all that flows from it; but also the Word of God, the life and light of God's grace, the gifts of the Spirit, the ministries of teaching, preaching and sanctifying. How often do we say 'That which unites us is more important than that which still divides us'. But do we really believe this and act upon it?

The second aspect of my ecumenical vision is rooted in the small things, the small gatherings, events and meetings in every locality. Jesus tells us that: 'Where two or three are gathered in my name, there I am in the midst of them' (Matthew 18:20). We need to encourage Christians in every village, town and city to share a common life, to do things together, to pray together, read the Gospels together, examine and reflect together on our world and the culture that surrounds us. It may be difficult, but in the words of Mother Teresa of Calcutta, 'God doesn't call me to be successful, he calls me to be faithful.' We, too, need to be faithful to our ecumenical obligation.

The Three Enemies of Ecumenism

The three enemies of ecumenism are suspicion, inertia and impatience.

Of these, the first enemy, suspicion, is perhaps the most difficult to eradicate. If my commitment to Christ has been as a Roman Catholic, and has been deep, secure and unaltered for decades, then dialogue, openness and reappraisal are likely to be unnerving and a breeding ground for fear and suspicion. If, on the other hand, my heritage has been within the Anglican Communion or one of the Free Churches, then it may be built into my heritage that there are many aspects of Roman Catholicism which are a betrayal of the Gospel. Am I not therefore going to find something suspicious in Rome's ecumenical advances? It is here that we have to trust in God and in one another.

There is no easy answer to the second enemy, the problem of inertia, except to assert that, for those of us who believe, there is no option but to go on in the conviction that this is the will of Christ. Some would say that the 'honeymoon' days of ecumenism are over, and the original glow has dimmed. There is no doubt that it can be hard to sustain ecumenical activity and concern when the churches are becoming increasingly concerned with their own internal tensions and challenges. But ecumenism is for each one of us. We constantly hunger for God and if we love him and seek him then we shall also want to do his will. I believe firmly that it is his will that we should become one as Christ is one with his father.

I suspect that we all suffer sometimes from the third enemy of ecumenism, impatience. There are Christians in all the Churches who say that the ecumenical movement is dragging its feet. Why argue about creed and authority? Why cannot all Christian Churches offer the Eucharist to everyone who believes that Christ becomes really present on the altar under the form of bread and wine? Why should doctrines seem to limit our love? But the work of reconciliation needs patience: that patience which is a quality of mind and of heart rather than a mere marking of time; a patience rooted in the profound belief that it is God who is in charge, that this is God's work, that it is his will and that it is he who accomplishes his gracious design through us, but in his own time.

Practising What We Preach

Ecumenism can of course only be fruitful where it is actually practised; when each of our communities gathers together with others to pray together, work together and witness together. Ecumenism starts in my local parish, in my own community. When Christians pray together we discover and deepen the conviction that we celebrate the same faith and the same Lord. In praying together and making friends with one another we discover that disunity between Christian churches cannot destroy the unity that is established by Christ between members of his Church, even if that Church is presently divided. When we work together to carry out the command to love our neighbour we realise that we seek to share the same faith and that we do share the same Spirit. The dimension of orthopraxy, or right practice, can take some of the strain out of matters of orthodoxy and can help to lessen the tension we experience in our present state of partial communion. In the Roman Catholic Church it is easy to think in terms only of the Mass and this is the area in which the painful division over the reception of the Eucharist is most evident. We need to be creative in arranging opportunities for non-eucharistic celebrations centred around the Word of God.

My prayer is that Christians will pray together, genuinely and humbly, really yearning to be more fully united in our one Lord. I want us to recognise that this cannot come about unless we have faith in the power of the Holy Spirit and understand that the Lord is truly present wherever there are two or three gathered in his name, and doubly present among his disciples praying for unity. I long for an ecumenism of friendship, because I have so often witnessed the power of those who extend their hands to one another because they are close in faith. All this hastens the day of reconciliation.

I had special experience of this during the sixteen years in which I was co-chairman of the Anglican–Roman Catholic International Commission (ARCIC). Year by year an equal number of Anglicans and Roman Catholics met together to study and to pray. During the time that we spent together we developed a common spirituality which helped to form a close bond of unity between us. While it is important to study together the doctrinal matters that may still divide us, it is even more important to develop the spiritual unity which is at the heart of the ecumenical movement.

In his 2003 encyclical letter *Ecclesia de Eucharistia* Pope John Paul II, while acknowledging the present limitations to eucharistic sharing, reaffirmed our ecumenical communion in prayer and spiritual desire when he quoted from *Ut Unum Sint*:

> And yet we have a burning desire to join in celebrating the one Eucharist of the Lord, and this desire itself is already a common prayer of praise, a single supplication. Together we speak to the Father and increasingly we do so 'with one heart'.[8]

I long to see Church leaders taking more risks and

creating the space for Christians to grow together and to be reconciled. I yearn for Christians to realise that they are in fact already in the process of reconciliation because the one Spirit of God is already working in their hearts. Once we understand this we are moved to a greater mutual love and a greater longing for unity, and we realise that we are travelling together as brothers and sisters on the road with no exit.

In 1523, writing to Christians in Riga and Tallin, Martin Luther reminded them that 'faith makes us joyful and at peace with God and it must make us love him, because we see that it is God's will and the gracious attitude of his favour towards us that causes Christ thus to deal with us.' If we could so live our faith as the beloved of Christ, and reflect Christ's joyfulness and peace, we would rediscover our confidence as messengers of the Gospel and as evangelisers, a confidence that makes us self-forgetful, ready to serve and ready to come together united beyond our differences.

In this context I remember with great fondness the May 2000 meeting of Anglican and Roman Catholic Bishops held in Canada at Mississauga, just west of Toronto. It was a unique occasion. The Archbishop of Canterbury, George Carey, and Cardinal Edward Cassidy, then president of the Pontifical Council for Promoting Christian Unity, had called together one Anglican and one Roman Catholic bishop from each of thirteen different countries and regions of the world where Anglicans and Roman Catholics live side by side in significant numbers.

We began the meeting with a sort of mini-retreat rather than a high-powered theological discussion. With the help of the Scriptures, some Church documents and music and song, we thought and prayed together about communion and our own daily need for conversion of heart. In a sense we had slowed down and focused on Christ, our common Lord. We were trying to respond to his prayer for the unity of his followers for which, as bishops, we have particular responsibility.

Mississauga was filled with a spirit of confidence and hope in the future. We were reminded in meditation that 'Our God is a God of surprises and he will always surprise us.' One day we will be surprised, even astonished, at the things God has brought about.

We are on a journey which we know will be fulfilled by the promptings of the Holy Spirit in the unity which is the will of Christ. Of that I am quite sure. If each one of us listens and tries to do the will of God in his or her life – if we do what Jesus teaches – then there is very good reason to believe that Christian unity will come about. Let us not be disheartened, even if we sometimes think that progress is slow. The previous Archbishop of Canterbury, George Carey, reminded us that the work of ecumenism is not just our work. It is the work of God and we have to plead with him to grace and bless our efforts.

When things were at a low ebb during the Second World War I was a young boy and I remember listening to a radio speech by Winston Churchill in the sitting room of my home in Reading. Churchill quoted from a poem by Arthur Hugh Clough: *Say Not the Struggle Naught Availeth*. I think it was the first piece of poetry I ever learnt by heart. I have always remembered the third verse:

> For while the tired waves, vainly breaking,
> Seem here no painful inch to gain,
> Far back, through creeks and inlets making,
> Comes silent, flooding in, the main.[9]

In the context of the ecumenical journey, the silent flood is the gifts of the Holy Spirit while the creeks and inlets are the coming together of Christians by God's work and God's will, not merely our own efforts.

The fact that Christians are united in this endeavour is of the greatest significance today. When Jesus and his disciples joined the wedding guests during the marriage feast at Cana the wine ran out – in part, perhaps, because Jesus had brought his friends along! Mary, the mother of Jesus, asked the help of her son and we are told that his initial response was perhaps somewhat reluctant: 'My time has not yet come.' His mother said to the servants, 'Do whatever he tells you.' Jesus told the servants to fill the jars with water – and it was changed into the finest wine.

The instruction 'Do whatever he tells you' applies also to us. Jesus tells us to be united. 'May they all be one,' he prayed, 'as you are in me, Father, and I in you, so that the world may believe it was you who sent me' (John 17:21). Ecumenism is a road with no exit. There is no way back. There is only completion. In the words of T. S. Eliot:

> With the drawing of this Love and the voice of this Calling
> We shall not cease from exploration
> And the end of all our exploring
> Will be to arrive where we started
> And know the place for the first time.[10]

CHAPTER SEVEN

A World Without a Father

The great crisis of humanity today is that it has lost its sense of the invisible. We have become experts in the visible, particularly in the West. If I was called upon to identify briefly the principal trait of the entire twentieth century I would be unable to find anything more precise and pithy than to repeat again and again, 'Men have forgotten God'. The failings of human consciousness deprived of its divine dimensions have been a determining factor in the major crimes of this century.

Alexander Solzhenitsyn[1]

My father was 32 when he married my mother, who was just 21. He qualified as a doctor in Cork and had come to England in the early years of the twentieth century. After various locum positions in the North of England, he eventually bought a medical practice in Reading. He had a struggle to build it up and never felt able to settle until he had paid off the debt on the practice and become established in the town. To 'settle down' in the Irish sense means to put down roots in your own place, with your own family and friends – to settle down in the place to which God has called you.

It was in this setting that I was born in 1932 and grew up

as the youngest of five boys, to be followed ten years later by a greatly welcomed girl. In many ways we were a very self-contained family. We lived in a large house which had belonged to a doctor for more than two hundred years, and which my mother must have had great difficulty in managing. Both my parents were anxious for their children to do well. My mother was particularly concerned that we should be well educated. She, like my father was Irish and, as I have mentioned, had studied French at University College in Cork. She decided that for one meal a day the conversation would be in French. I well remember those rather silent dinners with my mother trying to keep the French conversation going and the occasional muttered 'voulez-vous me passer les pommes de terre?' from one of the boys, followed by hoots of laughter all round.

Every year in August my father would take a house in the little Irish seaside village of Ardmore in County Waterford. On one occasion he sent three of my brothers aged 13, 12 and 10 ahead to cycle from Newport to Fishguard to catch the boat to Rosslare. It must have been well over 100 miles, so it took them several days, and they were only given sufficient money for one day at a time. They had to call at the post offices in Newport, Cardiff and Swansea in order to collect the money that my father had sent them *poste restante* to see them through the following day. Our anxious mother, awaiting news of her dear sons, at last received a postcard from Rosslare. She read it out: 'All sick, no money. Love, Jim'

Ours was a deeply Christian family. My father and mother attended Mass every morning and each evening before my father's surgery at six o'clock the whole family would kneel down and say the rosary together. Regular prayer, the Mass and other devotions of the Church were very much part of our life. It was always understood that religion was not only personal, but communal, and that our family was part of a much wider family which was the Church. We knew that we had an obligation to worship God, to love him and to make him known by the manner in which we lived. The gift of faith was deeply imprinted on our minds and our hearts.

'The Best of Times, the Worst of Times'

I mention something of my own background because I was extremely fortunate to be born into a loving family which gave me a sense of meaning – of 'home'. This sense of home and belonging is important for human flourishing. Sometimes I look around and wonder if we aren't living through an 'epoch of homelessness'. In spite of the massive achievements of the past century, there are signs that we have lost the sense of being 'at home' in a world that makes sense to us. During the past fifty years there has been greater scientific and technological progress than in the two previous millennia, and yet we are lost in a cosmos whose wonders we are only just beginning to understand.

The Jewish philosopher Martin Buber speaks of 'epochs of habitation' and 'epochs of homelessness':

> In the former, man lives in the world as in a house, as in a home. In the latter, man lives in the world as in an open field and at times he does not even have four pegs with which to set up a tent.[2]

Is it 'the best of times' as Charles Dickens put it in *A Tale of Two Cities*? In many ways it is. But perhaps it is also the 'worst of times', as the spiritual and moral values that underpin our human community have been so badly shaken. In 1940 teachers were asked to identify the most serious problems they faced in schools. The responses focused on such matters as talking out of turn, chewing gum, making a noise, running in the corridors, not wearing school uniform, and dropping litter. Today, the same question provokes responses focusing on drug and alcohol abuse, teenage pregnancy, suicide, depression, stress and disorientation.

I have said that I was extremely fortunate in being born into a loving family which gave me a sense of meaning. This, I think, touches the heart of the matter. Timothy Radcliffe has reminded us that the fundamental crisis of our society is perhaps one of meaning: 'Violence and corruption are symptoms of a deeper malady: the hunger for some meaning to our existence.'[3]

The Chief Rabbi, Jonathan Sacks, tells the story of a Jewish sage who, stroking his beard and looking up from his volume of the Talmud says, 'Thank God, things are so good.' Then he pauses and adds, 'But . . . if things are so good, how come they're so bad?' Rabbi Sacks continues,

> That, surely, is the question of our time. The Jewish answer is that in achieving material abundance we have lost our moral and spiritual bearings. In achieving technical mastery, we have lost sight of the question, To what end? Valuing science at the expense of ethics, we have unparalleled knowledge of what is, and unprecedented doubts about what ought to be.[4]

A Christian can only agree. There seems to me to be a deep unease lying at the heart of our Western civilisation. Alexander Solzhenitsyn spoke of this as the 'spiritual exhaustion of the West' which he attributed to the fact that we have placed human beings at the centre and pinnacle of reality. When he received the Templeton Prize for Progress in Religion in 1983 Solzhenitsyn told his audience: 'The great crisis of humanity today is that it has lost its sense of the invisible . . . "Men have forgotten God".'[5]

In Orthodox monasteries there is a lovely custom that at the end of the day, following Night Prayers, the Abbot sits in his chair and one by one his monks approach him and kneel before him. The Abbot kisses each monk on the head as a sign of forgiveness, a sign of acceptance, a sign of love.

This ritual places the members of the community in a particular relation to the Abbot. He is an 'abba', a Father who symbolically accepts and blesses each one of them in his weakness.

I believe that we do have a God who speaks to us about who we are, who shows us how we are to live and who receives and accepts our lives lovingly. By closing our minds and hearts to him we find ourselves living in a world without a Father. There is a great need for spiritual fatherhood in a society in which more and more families are broken, and in which fatherless families are becoming the norm rather than the exception. The children of God need to be born and fathered into the Kingdom. We need spiritual fathers to guide us and nurture us in the ways of God. There is a need for spiritual paternity today, just as there was among the ancient monks and nuns of the desert when a word from the spiritual father or mother could serve as a guiding light for months and years.

In our present 'epoch of homelessness' we need someone to guide us in how to exercise our freedom with responsibility and maturity. We need to be told that we matter, that we are forgiven and cherished. I am not talking about interference in our lives that would deny our freedom or make us continually dependent upon an authority that imprisons and stifles us, or that would deny our dignity as human beings. I am talking about our need for a God who speaks to us about who we are and about the ways that will lead us to a responsible exercise of our freedom. I am talking about our dignity as sons and daughters of the One who receives and accepts our lives with love. But if we close our hearts and minds to him, if we forget or exclude God, then our lives will lose their meaning.

In the Christian tradition this has been most profoundly manifested in the life of Jesus Christ. Jesus, 'who loved us and gave his life for us' as St Paul says, is God's word of love to us. In Jesus we see what kind of God our God is. In him we are able to recognise God: 'He who sees me sees the Father' (John 14:9), and at the same time we are able to say with him, 'Abba, Father'. Jesus left us the 'Our Father', the Lord's Prayer. It is the best known of all Christian prayers and expresses our faith and our trust in the God who loves us.

Whilst writing this I am conscious of the people I meet who find it difficult to call God 'Father' because their experience of human fatherhood has not been as rich or sustaining as my own. Sometimes personal experience of parents or of the absence of parents can make it difficult to believe in God or to trust in him. I understand something of their struggle, but I believe that each one of us can be freed by God from the limitations of our own history to make Jesus' prayer our prayer, so that we can continually learn to trust the God who created us.

In the Hebrew Bible which Christians know as the Old Testament and which we treasure and venerate alongside our Jewish brothers and sisters there are many rich and suggestive images that can help us to enter in to a profound relationship of trust with God. In the writings of the prophets images of mothers, midwifes, nurses, and a mother bird spreading her wings protectively and lovingly over her young are all used to help us imagine God's caring love for us. In the Gospels, too, Jesus gives us many examples and images which speak of God's search for us. In chapter 15 of Luke's Gospel he tells three stories which speak to us of the tender love and reaching out of God to us his children: the parables of the prodigal son, the good shepherd and the lost coin.

We are all familiar with the parable of the good shepherd. He loves his sheep so much that when one is lost he leaves the other ninety-nine to search for it; and he perseveres until he finds it. That parable sits in the gospel alongside the vivid and telling story of the woman who loses one of her ten coins. We all know what it is like when we lose something precious, or something we really need. For me, all too often it is a book I am reading or a text that I have prepared for a homily or for a talk. And when I lose my glasses as well, everything else is put aside until I have found the book, the text or the glasses. The search becomes all-consuming. The woman in the parable is like that. She leaves everything she is doing and searches the whole house, from top to bottom, until she finds her missing coin. When she finds it she calls in her neighbours and shares her joyful discovery with them. The gospel doesn't tell us this, but you can just imagine the woman and her neighbours having something to eat and drink while they share the woman's relief and satisfaction, and laughing and chattering together, happy that their friend's search has proved fruitful.

The shepherd looking for the lost sheep and the woman searching for her lost coin are both images of God's search for us. Each parable in its own way expresses the same truth; we are so precious to God that God will search for us until we are found, whatever we have done and wherever we have gone. These wonderful images help us understand the way God regards you and me, and the way he regards all the brothers and sisters who share our planet. Ultimately, the mystery of God is beyond all our images and concepts. But one truth stands out: God loves us and searches for us, and it is in responding to God's presence and love that our lives find their meaning.

God is Spirit, neither male nor female, and creator of both men and women in the divine image. Our metaphors for God are always limited and God, the ultimate reality, can never be fully grasped in language. I love the prayer of St Gregory Nazianzen, written in the fourth century:

You who are beyond anything, are not these words all that can be sung about you? What hymn could tell about you, what language? No word can express you. What could our

mind cling to? You are beyond any intelligence. Only you
are the unutterable for all that is uttered comes from you.
Those who speak and those who are silent proclaim you.
Universal desire, universal groaning calls you . . . Have
mercy, you who are beyond anything.

I am conscious that we find the truth of God's inexhaustible
love difficult to accept. Over the past three centuries the
human race, led by the West, has made astonishing scientific and technological leaps. In doing so it has brushed
aside the question of God as something that stands in the
way of human progress. Many dismiss religious belief in
God as incredible or irrelevant, or regard God as too far
away to be contemplated anyway. There is a view, held by
some of our contemporaries, that belief in God places limitations on our freedom. I believe the contrary to be the case.
I see God as grounding and guaranteeing our freedom. I see
the recognition of God as inseparably connected with the
recognition of human dignity and human rights.

Pope John Paul II has insisted throughout his long
pontificate that since we constitute ourselves by our actions,
we must be free. Called by God to loving communion with
him and with one another, it is only through the exercise of
our freedom that we can respond to God's call. By a responsible use of our own freedom we make ourselves the kind of
persons that we are called to be. All of this is explained in
Pope John Paul's magnificent encyclical letter, *Veritatis
Splendor*. In his biography of the Pope George Weigel puts it
like this:

> What passes for moral argument on the edge of the
> twenty-first century is too often vast confusion. Terms like
> 'right' and 'wrong', 'virtue' and 'duty' are bandied about
> with no common understanding of what they mean. One
> group's abomination is another's basic human right.
> What some consider acts of mercy, others regard as homi-
> cides for the sake of convenience. When it comes to moral

argument, the modern world too often plays the role of that classic cynic, Pontius Pilate, with his dismissive question, 'Truth'? What is 'truth'? (John 18:38). Pilate, and many self-consciously modern people, think that question is the end of the debate. In *Veritatis Splendor*, John Paul suggests that it is really the beginning.

The widespread notion that freedom can be lived without reference to binding moral truths is another unique characteristic of contemporary life. From Mount Sinai (where the Ten Commandments were understood to be the moral conditions for Israel living its freedom) to the U.S. Declaration of Independence (which staked the American claim to independent nationhood on certain 'self-evident' moral truths), it had been widely understood that freedom and truth had a lot to do with each other. No more. And the uncoupling of freedom from truth, led in one, grim direction. Freedom, detached from truth, becomes license, and license becomes freedom's undoing. Without any common understanding of moral truth, life is reduced to the assertion of everyone's will-to-power. That, in turn, leads to chaos. And since human beings fear chaos above all, they will reach for the chains of tyranny to bring order back into life. Freedom untethered from truth is its own mortal enemy.

The idea that every human being creates his or her own truth – what is true 'for me' – is yet another crucial factor in contemporary moral confusions. The modern or 'postmodern' variation on this perennial temptation is the claim that every moral system is a cultural construct 'all the way down'. I may think that I value freedom and that 'freedom' has some objective meaning. In thinking that, according to postmodern theorists, I am deluding myself, for my concept of 'freedom' is as 'culturally constructed' as someone else's claim that child sacrifice is a grand idea.

Against such deconstructions of the moral drama of the human condition, Pope John Paul II in *Veritatis Splendor* insists that we are truly free and that our freedom is the condition for any serious concept of 'morality'.[6]

Pope John Paul's convictions about freedom and truth resonate with my experience and my reflection on that experience. Many people in our society seek to quench their thirst for freedom with possessions and experiences which they believe will satisfy their deepest needs – the 'freedom' of the market place, the 'freedom' of the consumer society. But it is becoming increasingly clear that an exclusive reliance on the market place does in the end actually prevent us from taking our destiny into our own hands, from taking a firm hold upon our own lives and future and growing into the men and women, the free and fully human persons, we are called to become.

As we become richer, more able to possess what we want when we want it, we do not necessarily appear to become happier. Within our society material conditions have certainly improved, but the quality of our lives has coarsened. The pictures of beauty, wealth and fame that smile out at us from our television screens and the billboards on every corner cannot be taken at face value. Only too often they are merely masks that hold out promises they are unable to fulfil. The acquisition of enormous wealth, unbridled sexual gratification and the endless accumulation of power do not, as the experience of those who have pursued or acquired these things seem to tell us, of themselves bring fulfilment to the human heart, or automatically produce a civilised society.

I remember visiting South America on numerous occasions when priests from the Arundel and Brighton diocese were working there. What a contrast. I do not want to idealise countries which are wrestling with serious social problems or where there is an urgent need to expand the opportunities and improve the quality of life for the poor. Nevertheless, the people I met in Peru displayed, amidst the simplicity of their lives, an extraordinary contentment and sense of gratitude; gratitude, not least, for their faith. Too much money can cripple joy and freedom. Wealth, self-gratification and power can become idols. In greedily grasping them, we risk becoming enslaved by them – the very opposite of the liberation and fulfilment for which the human heart longs.

There is a danger in our Western world of becoming consumed by consumerism. Many parents fear that their children are being 'designer fashioned' by advertisers and by the things that money can buy. It is surely a de-moralised society where the only good is the 'good' that I want, the only rights are my own rights, and the only life with meaning and value is the life I want for myself.

The ideal of life that Jesus Christ holds out to us stands in stark contrast to this. Jesus is, in the famous words of Dietrich Bonhoeffer, 'the man for others'. The meaning of the life of Jesus lies in his response to his Father's love for him, a response that meant that his life was given for us:. 'What greater love can a man have than this: to lay down his life for his friends.'

My reflection on this reality is drawn from my own experience of faith. My faith is the greatest treasure that my parents bequeathed to me and the central aim of my life has always been to share this treasure. If, as I have suggested, the fundamental malady in our society is the unsatisfied hunger for some meaning to our existence, our healing lies in coming to know that God, the Creator of all that is, loves us unconditionally. That is the treasure that was bequeathed to me. God puts no conditions on his love for us. It is not like a qualified or a grudging, 'If you are a good girl or a good boy, I will love you'. No, it is an unequivocal statement, a word pledged to us by God that will never be taken back. God, St John tells us, has so loved the world that he has sent his only Son that we might have the fullness of life. That is, quite simply, the truth and the deepest meaning of our existence. We are loved by God and we are each called, together with all the brothers and sisters who share our pilgrimage, to a communion of life with God.

I am acutely aware as I write this of something that will probably be in the mind of many readers. How do we reconcile this image of God, this view of God's relationship with us and with the world, with the existence of suffering and evil? The problem of evil is indeed one of the main stumbling-blocks to a religious view of the world. It is a stumbling-block that some who have experienced the effects of physical suffering or moral evil in their own lives, or in the lives of those whom they love, are unable to overcome. I have no simple or glib answer to the problem of evil. The question is central and it is vast. I would simply mention Dostoevsky's great novel, *The Brothers Karamazov*, where the novelist raises the question of evil and suffering in a way that anyone who reads the novel can never forget. Dostoevsky does not offer a response at the level of understanding, but chooses rather to respond at the practical and existential level, with the offer of dedicated self-sacrificial love.

There is a famous passage in which the Grand Inquisitor condemns his prisoner (Jesus) for allowing evil and for giving to his creatures the freedom to do such terrible things.

When the Inquisitor finished speaking, he waited for some time for the Prisoner's reply. His silence distressed him. He saw that the Prisoner had been listening intently to him all the time, looking gently into his face and evidently not wishing to say anything in reply. The old man would have liked him to say something, however bitter and terrible. But he suddenly approached the old man and softly kissed him gently on his bloodless, aged lips. That was all his answer.[7]

The God who created this world does not abandon it.

Instead he comes into it in the person of Jesus and as we ponder the mystery of suffering, sin and death we must continue to direct our gaze towards Jesus who was born in Bethlehem and died on a cross. God is not indifferent to our suffering or to our sins but instead becomes himself the victim of evil in order to overcome it. In order to believe this we need to have faith; which means that we have to trust. And to trust someone is to believe that their word is reliable and that their life is one of integrity.

We are faced with the paradox of religious pluralism, with many rival and incompatible claims to the truth. This is not new. In the Acts of the Apostles St Paul debates with the Athenians about the panoply of Gods (Acts 17:16–32). Paul points to the empty plinth among the sacred statues which carries the inscription 'To an unknown God'. He explains that this 'unknown' God is the God who he is now proclaiming to them. Paul argues that the God who gives life and breath to everyone has been revealing himself throughout human history and has revealed himself uniquely and supremely in the person of Christ. In his debate with the philosophers of Athens Paul appeals to their reason in support of his own faith. That which he advocates he also proposes as objectively true.

We all seek meaning and purpose, and I believe that on our spiritual journey we are constantly being led towards a deeper understanding of the truth that lies beyond our present grasp. The invitation to follow Jesus is an invitation to lifelong exploration in search of the ultimate truth with the person of Jesus as our guide. To believe in him is not to act in defiance of reason and rationality. Rather it is an invitation to discover the truth, to find the most fulfilling way to live in the complex world of the twenty-first century.

This was much in evidence during the hugely popular 'Seeing Salvation' exhibition of paintings at the National Gallery in London in 2000, and in the success of the accompanying television broadcasts. Hundreds of thousands of people of no formal religious belief still want to be in touch with the great art that only a religious culture can produce. The face of Jesus is the face of God made flesh amongst us, healing and saving us; but it is also the face of humanity. It is Jesus who reveals us to ourselves. When we see Jesus we are seeing ourselves, infinitely loved and cherished by God and drawn throughout our lives towards the blessed peace of the Resurrection. We see our true worth, the fact that we are worthy of such infinite pains on the part of God. In our hearts we long for this, and in Jesus we see that it is true.

Every year, during Holy Week, I love to read, slowly and meditatively, chapters 13–17 of St John's Gospel. Here we find the prayer of Jesus to God his Father, on the night before he died. The words of Jesus mirror our own desires and struggles and hopes. They also mirror the eternal conversation that takes place in God and into which as his sons and daughters we are brought.

God is the giver, and we and the world are the gift. It is only before this mystery that we come to understand ourselves. When God reveals himself to Moses in the burning bush at Mount Horeb the first question that Moses puts to God is, 'Who Am I?' Not, 'Who are you?', but 'Who Am I?' It is only in the presence of God who is greater than everything, that we come to an understanding of ourselves: when we are outside that divine presence we find ourselves 'parentless' like homeless children.

Psychologists tell us that a child's most basic need is for a sense of security. Later on the growing child will need to develop a sense of self-esteem, of self-worth and sound love of self. These needs underline the vital importance of the family as a stable, loving unit to which we can belong. From the beginning God created male and female, in a relation of partnership. The family is the basic cell of society and we must do what we can to avoid its breakdown. It is vitally important that the family in its fundamental form, namely the married couple and the nuclear family, is not further undermined. It is within the family that each generation passes on its values and so ensures the continuity of civilisation. The family is the crucible of society's future; it is a force that humanises society and counteracts the depersonalising influences of so much in our world. The condition of being 'at home' in the world begins with being 'at home' in the stability and loving commitment of a family. It is a condition of genuine humanity that our relationships of love are relationships of stability. As adults too we need the assurance that we are recognised, affirmed and wanted, and that our lives have meaning and purpose.

The 'family', of course, is a concept which, while conveying the basic ideal of a mother and father with their children, takes on various forms in different cultures. Besides the basic unit of the nuclear family, the extended family, with grandparents, in-laws, uncles, aunts and cousins is still very strong in some countries. There are also single-parent families, where for a variety of reasons, including death, physical separation, divorce, or the special situation of unmarried parents who nevertheless have the courage to bring their child into the world, a single parent raises their children without the support of a life-partner. I have known many such situations and I want to express my respect and admiration for the sense of responsibility, the persevering dedication, and the self-sacrificing love that I have seen in many single-parent families. Single-parent families very often require support, both physical and emotional, from the wider community. Our church communities, while dedicated to fostering the model of the full family, must also lead the way in sustaining and supporting single-parent families. Every family, however large or small, faces the challenging and enormously important task of raising children who are capable of realising their God-given potential to choose freely to commit themselves to that which is true and good, and to become people who seek to enter into communion with others and to give themselves in service and love.

The most important service we can offer to our brothers and sisters, whatever their situation, is to show that they, and we, are loved, in all our weakness. Unless we have this fundamental assurance it is difficult to reach out towards a higher ideal. Timothy Radcliffe puts it very well:

> The moral teaching of the Church should never consist in telling people that they should not love someone. It should only invite them to love better. There is no human love that is not in need of healing, which does not need to be led to maturity and fullness. That applies to married couples too. If we wish to show that the Church's moral teaching is good news, we have to be with people, enter their homes, enjoy their friendship. We have to understand how they see the world, learn what they have to teach us, see through their eyes, grow in mutual trust. God's friendship with the human race is the very heart of the gospel. So we cannot express our deepest moral convictions except in a context of friendship.[8]

Whether it is as children or as adults, in the nuclear family, the extended family, the single-parent family, or in the networks of relationships that sometimes serve to substitute for families, all relationships find their bedrock and their ultimate reference point in the assurance that God, the very ground of our being, loves us with unfailing love. The world does not lie abandoned, without unconditional love. God so loved the world that he sent his only Son that we might share communion of life together in and with him.

NOTES

Chapter One: A Pilgrim's Journey

1 *Gaudium et Spes* (Pastoral Constitution on the Church in the Modern World, 1965), art. 1
2 Cardinal Basil Hume, *To Be a Pilgrim* (London: St Paul Publications, 1984), p. 37
3 Gerard W. Hughes, *In Search of a Way* (London: Darton, Longman & Todd, 1986)
4 Robert Blair Kaiser, *Inside the Council* (London: Burns and Oates, 1963)
5 Pope John XXIII, *Journal of a Soul* (London: Geoffrey Chapman, 1959)
6 Yves Congar, tr. Donald Attwater, *Lay People in the Church* (London: Geoffrey Chapman, 1957)
7 Hume, *To Be a Pilgrim*, p. 38
8 Cardinal Leon-Joseph Suenens, *Journey of a Soul* (London: Geoffrey Chapman, 1984), p. 415
9 Pope John XXIII, Opening address to the Second Vatican Council, October 1962, tr. Walter Abbot sj, *The Documents of Vatican II* (London: Geoffrey Chapman, 1967), p. 715
10 Ibid., p. 717
11 Ibid., p. 712
12 Pope Paul VI, from a sermon in Manila during his visit to the Philippines, 29 November 1970

113

Chapter Two: Community and Communion

1 Jean Vanier, *Community and Growth* (London: Darton, Longman & Todd, 1979), p. 17

2 Henri de Lubac, *Catholicism* (New York: Sheed & Ward, 1958), p. 131

3 *Lumen Gentium* (Dogmatic Constitution on the Church, 1964), art. 1

4 Ibid., art. 48

5 Pope John Paul II, *Relationes Finalis*, Second Extraordinary General Assembly of the Synod, 24 November–8 December 1985

6 *Lumen Gentium*, art. 48

7 Pope John Paul II, *Novo Millennio Ineunte* (2000), art. 43

8 Quoted in Malcolm Muggeridge, *Something Beautiful for God* (London: Fontana, 1986), p. 38

9 *Sacrosanctum Concilium* (Constitution on the Sacred Liturgy, 1963), art. 7

10 Ibid., art. 10

11 Pope John Paul II, *Dominicae Cenae* (1980), art. 13

12 Pope John Paul II, *Ecclesia de Eucharistia* (On the Eucharist and the Church, 2003)

13 *Gaudium et Spes* (Pastoral Constitution on the Church in the Modern World, 1965), art. 24

Chapter Three: Being Faithful

1 Jean Vanier, *Community and Growth* (London: Darton, Longman & Todd, 1979), p. 31

2 Timothy Garton Ash, *The File* (London: Flamingo, 1997), p. 226

3 Karol Wojtyla, *Sign of Contradiction* (London: St Paul's Publications, 1979), p. 140

4 Isaiah Berlin, *Personal Impressions* (New York: Viking Press, 1981), pp. 150–1

5 *Gaudium et Spes* (Pastoral Constitution on the Church in the Modern World, 1965), art. 16

6 Vanier, *Community and Growth*, p. 31

Chapter Four: Openness of Heart

1 Douglas Coupland, *Life after God* (New York, Simon & Schuster, 1994), p. 359
2 *The Rule of St Benedict*, ch. 3
3 *Young People in a Changing Europe: School of Faith* (CCEE working document for 10th Symposium of European Bishops, 24-28 April 2002)
4 Pope John Paul II, *Redemptor Hominis* (1979), ch. 3, para 4
5 Pope John Paul II, *Novo Millennio Ineunte* (2000), paras 43–44
6 Ibid., para 46

Chapter Five: Living Authority

1 Timothy Radcliffe OP, Address to the Second Synod of Bishops in Europe, October 1999
2 *Lumen Gentium* (Dogmatic Constitution on the Church, 1963), art. 9
3 *The Sign We Give* (Report from the Working Party for Collaborative Ministry issued by the Roman Catholic Bishops' Conference of England and Wales, 1999)
4 *Dei Verbum* (Dogmatic Constitution on Divine Revelation, 1965), art. 8
5 Ibid., art. 10
6 Pope John Paul II, *Ut Unum Sint* (1995), art. 95
7 Synod of Bishops, 'Jesus Christ Alive in His Church, Source of Hope for Europe' (Second Special Assembly for Europe, 1999) para. 31

Chapter Six: Unity in the Truth

1 Pope John Paul II, Address at Canterbury Cathedral, 1982
2 Norman Goodall, *Second Fiddle* (London: SPCK, 1997), p. 146
3 Common Declaration of His Holiness Paul VI and His Grace Michael Ramsey, Archbishop of Canterbury at the Monastery of St Paul, 24 March 1966

4 *The Pope in Britain: the Complete Texts* (London: Catholic Truth Society, 1985)

5 *Unitatis Redintegratio* (Decree on Ecumenism of the Second Vatican Council (1964), art. 4

6 Pope John Paul II, *Ut Unum Sint* (1995), art. 95

7 Thérèse Vanier, foreword to *Nick, Man of the Heart* (Dublin: Gill and Macmillan, 1993), p. xiv

8 Pope John Paul II, *Ut Unum Sint*, quoted in Pope John Paul II, *Ecclesia de Eucharistia* (On the Eucharist and the Church, 2003), para. 44

9 Arthur Hugh Clough, *Say Not the Struggle Naught Availeth* (1849). (First published under the title *The Struggle* in *The Crayon*, August 1855)

10 T. S. Eliot, 'Little Gidding' from *Four Quartets* in *Collected Poems* (London: Faber and Faber, 1974), p. 222

Chapter Seven: A World Without a Father

1 Alexander Solzhenitsyn, Address on receiving the Templeton Prize for Progress in Religion, 1983

2 Martin Buber, *Between Man and Man* (Boston: Beacon Press, 1947), p. 126

3 Timothy Radcliffe OP, *Sing a New Song: The Christian Vocation* (Dublin: Dominican Publications), p. 129

4 Jonathan Sacks, *Radical Then, Radical Now: The Legacy of the World's Oldest Religion* (London: HarperCollins, 2001), p. 68

5 Solzhenitsyn, Address on receiving the Templeton Prize

6 George Weigel, *Witness to Hope: The Biography of Pope John Paul II* (London: HarperCollins, 1999), p. 689

7 Fyodor Dostoevsky, *The Brothers Karamazov* (London: Penguin Classics, 1993), ch. 5

8 Timothy Radcliffe OP, *I Call You Friends* (London: Continuum, 2003), p. 66